Fugitives & Refugees

1. *Geek Love* Written Here
2. Le Happy
3. Chuck Lived Here
4. The Feral Cat Races
5. Underground Kayaking
6. Hotel Rajneesh
7. Exotic Wednesday
8. Psycho Safeway
9. Piss-U
10. Piggott's Folly
11. Chuck Worked Here
12. Pull My Finger
13. Three Groins in a Fountain
14. Eviction Court
15. The Haunted Photograph
16. Nordies
17. Chuck Got Beat Up Here
18. Leprechaun Park
19. Scum Center
20. U.S.S. *Blueback*
21. Kidd Toy Museum
22. Haunted Bathrooms
23. Miss Mona's Rack
24. Vacuum Cleaner Museum
25. Satan's City
26. Bear Hunting
27. Darcelle XV
28. The Shanghai Tunnels
29. Hoodoo Antiques
30. Big Pink
31. American Advertising Museum
32. 24 Hour Church of Elvis (closed)
33. Powell's City of Books
34. Zippers Down
35. The Silver Dildo
36. The "Louie Louie" Building
37. Alimony Flats

Fugitives & Refugees

A WALK IN
PORTLAND, OREGON

Chuck Palahniuk

CROWN JOURNEYS

CROWN PUBLISHERS · NEW YORK

Title spread photographs by Chuck Palahniuk (Santa) and
© Macduff Everton/CORBIS (24 Hour Church of Elvis)

Grateful acknowledgment is made for permission to reprint the following
    material to:
Anton Pace and Delta Café, for the recipes "Fritters," "Fritter Dip," and "Black-
    Eyed Peas." Reprinted by permission of the Delta Café.
Le Happy Bar, Inc., for the recipe "Faux Vegan Crepes." Copyright © 2002 by
    Le Happy Bar, Inc. Reprinted by permission of Le Happy Bar, Inc.
Michael Cox and Wild Abandon, for the recipe "Dean Blair's Lemon-Lavender
    Scones." Reprinted by permission of Michael Cox and Wild Abandon.

Published by Crown Journeys, an imprint of Crown Publishers, New York.
Member of the Crown Publishing Group, a division of Random House, Inc.
www.randomhouse.com

CROWN JOURNEYS and the Crown Journeys colophon are trademarks of
Random House, Inc.

Printed in the United States of America

Design by Lauren Dong

Map by Jackie Aher

Library of Congress Cataloging-in-Publication Data
Palahniuk, Chuck.
    Fugitives and refugees : a walk in Portland, Oregon / Chuck
Palahniuk.— 1st ed.
    1. Portland (Or.)— Tours.   2. Alternative lifestyles— Oregon—
Portland—Guidebooks.   3. Curiosities and wonders—Oregon—Portland—
Guidebooks.   4. Walking—Oregon—Portland—Guidebooks.   I. Title.
    F884.P83 P35   2003
    917.95'490444—dc21   2002154008

ISBN 1-4000-4783-8

20 19 18 17 16 15 14 13 12

First Edition

For my grandmother, Ruth Tallent

1920–2002

Contents

CONTENTS

Fugitives & Refugees

INTRODUCTION: UNRAVELING THE FRINGE

"*E*VERYONE IN PORTLAND is living a minimum of three lives," says Katherine Dunn, the author of *Geek Love*. She says, "Everyone has *at least* three identities."

She's sitting in the window of her apartment in Northwest Portland, rolling cigarettes and smoking them, her long blond hair parted in the middle and tied back. She's wearing black-framed glasses. The radiators clank and a siren goes by, four stories below on Glisan Street.

"They're a grocery store checker, an archaeologist, and a biker guy," she says. "Or they're a poet, a drag queen, and a bookstore clerk."

Rolling another cigarette, she says, "It's tricky because all the rich people are in disguise. You never know when the scruffy guy across the counter could be someone rich enough to buy the store, chew it up, and spit it out."

Smoking, she says, "The nice little old ladies from the West Hills—with their sweater sets and pearls—they're all rabid advocates of the death penalty."

Those green, wooded hills fill the window behind her.

Art and bookshelves fill the walls. The rooms are painted heavy gem colors of deep red and green. Yellow freesia bloom in a vase on the dining room table. In the kitchen, hanging above the sink, is a framed photograph of Katherine's maternal grandmother, Tressie, who cooked for a railroad crew, working her way west through the Dakotas at age eighteen.

Katherine's theory is that everyone looking to make a new life migrates west, across America to the Pacific Ocean. Once there, the cheapest city where they can live is Portland. This gives us the most cracked of the crackpots. The misfits among misfits.

"We just accumulate more and more strange people," she says. "All we are are the fugitives and refugees."

In 1989, when she wrote her bestselling novel *Geek Love,* Katherine set the story in Portland. The novel—about an outcast circus sideshow family who work to have mutated, birth-defected children to boost their ticket sales—is easily the most famous book that uses the city as a background. Katherine wanted her story set in a place without associations in people's minds.

"When I was a young woman in Paris," she says, "I couldn't walk through the city and see it without seeing it the way the Impressionists did. Because I'd seen it through their eyes, it was impossible to see it any other way."

The genesis of *Geek Love* was here. One day Katherine's seven-year-old son, Ben, refused to walk with her through the International Rose Test Gardens, so she walked alone among the hybrid roses. "I thought to myself, 'These would not have occurred in nature—I should've *designed* a better child.'"

She swam in the basement pool at the Metropolitan Learning Center, swimming and writing the book in her mind. For years she wrote "The Slice," a weekly newspaper column that documented oddball Portland happenings.

Now, Portland has its own identity, she says. "It's no longer this blank look when someone says Portland or Seattle or Walla Walla."

Now Katherine Dunn is working on a new book. *Geek Love* is being reissued, for a new generation of fans. Still, she's not planning to leave.

"First of all," she says, "I can't drive. Besides, when you walk down the street, every corner has a story." She smokes, exhaling out the window above Glisan Street. "Here," she says, "the rolling history of your life is visible to you everywhere you look."

AND KATHERINE'S RIGHT. Every corner does have a story. And every hillside.

In 1980, six days after graduating from high school, I moved to Portland, to the Burlingame View Apartments, on a steep hillside covered with blackberry vines above the Burlingame Fred Meyer supermarket on SW Barbur Boulevard.

My two roommates work in restaurants, and our closet space is filled with boxes of stolen food. Cases of champagne. Three-gallon cans of escargot packed in olive oil. We buy our dope from a potter who lives on NE Killingsworth

Street and works in his basement, stoned and throwing the same coffee mug fifty times each day. Around him are racks filled with hundreds of identical coffee mugs, waiting to be fired in his kiln. He must be twenty-five or twenty-six years old. Ancient.

Days, I'm working as a messenger, delivering advertising proofs for the *Oregonian* newspaper. Nights, I wash dishes at Jonah's seafood restaurant. My roommates come home, and we throw food at each other. One night, cherry pie, big sticky red handfuls of it. We're eighteen years old. Legal adults. So we're stoned and drinking champagne every night, microwaving our escargot. Living it up.

In a moment of sacrifice, I find my childhood tonsils in a jar of formaldehyde with a label from Our Lady of Lourdes Hospital. In a grand gesture, I make a wish and throw the sealed jar off our apartment balcony, into the blackberry briars that cover the hillside.

It used to be easy when friends or family came to visit Portland. First, you took them to the Van Calvin Mannequin Museum. There they saw hundreds of dusty mannequins, arranged in nightmare settings in a sweltering hot warehouse. My favorite was the room where seventy battered, naked children sat watching black-and-white cartoons on a huge console television.

Then you visited the 24 Hour Church of Elvis, where tourists were married and publicly humiliated by the minister. Then the Western Bigfoot Society. Then the UFO Museum. Maybe you went to see the strippers at the old Carriage Room. Or you drove people out to the Safari

Club so they could see the dozens of rare tigers and lions and leopards, now stuffed and filthy with cigarette smoke in a disco. Maybe you went to an ORGASM party (Oregon Guild Activists of S&M), where you watched bondage and torture demos. After that, you took everybody for a ride on Samtrak: the World's Smallest Railway, and by then the weekend was pretty much over.

Those were the good old days, when Ronald Reagan and George Bush (the elder) dreaded coming here so much they called Portland "Little Beirut." A presidential whistle-stop meant anarchists would gather along SW Broadway, outside the president's suite in the Hilton Hotel. They'd eat mashed potatoes, regular white ones, or potatoes dyed red or blue with food coloring. Then, when the motorcade arrived, they drank Syrup of Ipecac and puked big Red, White, and Blue barf puddles all over the hotel.

Okay, okay, what nobody knew is stomach acid makes blue food coloring turn green. So it looked like a protest against Italy . . . It's the *thought* that counts.

Sigh.

The only trouble with the fringe is, it does tend to unravel.

Now Portland is the home of Tonya Harding and Bob Packwood. To FBI experts who profile serial killers, the Pacific Northwest is "America's Killing Fields," because the people are so friendly and trusting. The wilderness is always nearby. It rains, and things rot fast.

What follows are sort-of snapshots of Portland. A sort-of photo album of the moment. From ax murders to penguins with a shoe fetish. From underground opium dens to riding fire engines to live sex shows. These are the stories you won't find in any official Portland history book. From rampaging Santa Clauses to the Self-Cleaning House. Here's just the tip of the Portland, Oregon, iceberg. Myths. Rumors. Ghost stories. Recipes. What follows is a little history, a little legend, and a lot of friendly, sincere, fascinating people who maybe should've kept their mouths shut.

In between the people to meet and places to go, you'll find postcards. These aren't from places so much as from specific Portland moments.

My first apartment, for example, there on Barbur Boulevard. Within a month, one roommate got his third drunk driving arrest and fled to Seattle to avoid doing jail time. The other roommate fell in love with a Swedish woman who gave him a gold coke spoon with a ruby chip in the handle, and they went off to get married.

My three lives were messenger-dishwasher-stoner until the night two men robbed Jonah's seafood restaurant. They have pillowcases over their heads and sawed-off shotguns and make me press my face into the parking lot until my forehead is one big purple bruise. The restaurant owner wants me to double the amount stolen when I tell the police so he can turn a big profit on insurance fraud. For once I tell the truth, and I get fired.

I give up the apartment and move into a rented room.

Still, somewhere on that steep hillside of maple trees and blackberry stickers, my tonsils are where I threw them. The wish I made was to someday be a writer.

Talk the Talk:
A Portland Vocabulary Lesson

Y OU SAY, "OR-GAWN." I say, "OR-a-gen." Nothing—
short of a California license plate—marks you as an
outsider faster than how you mispronounce local words.
Here's a quick guide to local slang and how to say words
such as *Willamette, Multnomah,* and *Couch.*

Alimony Flats/Empty-Nest Flats: See the Pearl
District.

Ban Roll-on Building: The nickname for the building
at 1000 SW Broadway. With the Broadway Metroplex
Theaters in its basement, the building's nickname
comes from what looks like a short, pale dome on
the roof.

Benson Bubblers: The nickname for the elaborate
four-armed public drinking fountains on downtown
streets, originally donated by lumber tycoon Simon
Benson.

Big Pink: The tallest building in Portland, the forty-three-story U.S. Bancorp Tower at W Burnside Street and SW Fifth Avenue.

The Black Box: The international-style 200 SW Market Street building.

Blue Jean: The nickname for Eugene, the home of the liberal arts University of Oregon.

The Bore-egonian: A nickname for the daily *Oregonian* newspaper.

Choirboys Peeing: A nickname for the fountain consisting of five arcs of spurting pipe at the corner of W Burnside Street and SW Fifth Avenue. It's also known as "the Carwash."

Corn Valley: The nickname for Corvallis, the home of Oregon State University, the state agricultural school.

Couch: Pronounced "Kooch," it's a street that runs through Northwest and Northeast Portland, named for Oregonian pioneer Captain John H. Couch.

Cruising the Gut: Teenagers cruising in a loop through downtown, going south on SW Broadway and north on SW Fourth Avenue.

The Devil's Triangle: The triangle formed by W Burnside Street and SW Stark and Eleventh. Occupied for years by the Silverado bar and the Club Portland men's bathhouse.

Enema 21: What employees call the Cinema 21 theater, on NW Twenty-first Avenue.

Estée Lauder's: A nickname for the gay bar C. C. Slaughter's.

Felony Flats: The neighborhood of Southeast Portland bounded by SE Foster Road, the 205 freeway, and Johnson Creek Boulevard, known for having Portland's highest density of drug labs and ex-convict residents.

The Flesh Grotto: A nickname for the Fish Grotto restaurant, from when it was a popular singles' meat market, where Katherine Dunn (author of *Geek Love*) worked as a cocktail waitress.

Garlic Gulch: The neighborhood formerly dominated by Italian businesses along the south side of SE Belmont Street near Eleventh Avenue.

The Ghetto: The interconnected bars and dance clubs that surround the Fish Grotto restaurant at SW Eleventh Avenue and Stark Street.

Glisan: Originally pronounced "GLISS-en," currently pronounced "GLEE sin," a street running through Northwest and Northeast Portland, named for pioneer Dr. Rodney Glisan.

Hotel Rajneesh: The redbrick building at SW Eleventh Avenue and Main Street, formerly the Martha Washington Hotel for Women, currently a Multnomah County jail. It was owned by the cult followers of the Bhagwan Shree Rajneesh in the 1980s.

The Jail Blazers: The local NBA team, the Portland Trailblazers. A nickname that stuck after several players were arrested for a variety of crimes.

Lake No-Negro/Fake Lost Ego/Fake Oswego: Nicknames for Lake Oswego, an affluent bedroom community south of Portland.

"Louie Louie" Building: The building at 409 SW Thirteenth Avenue where the Kingsmen originally recorded the song "Louie Louie." A local production company, Food Chain Films, occupies the preserved recording studio on the second floor. The brass plaque marking the building has been stolen.

Menopause Manor: The Ione Plaza apartment building near Portland State University, especially since 1985.

Multnomah: Pronounced "Mult-NO-mah," from the native word *Nematlnomacqu,* the name of a tribe the Lewis and Clark Expedition found camped on what is now Sauvie Island. The name of the county that comprises most of Portland.

Murphy & Finnegan: An old nickname for the Meier & Frank department store, downtown at SW Fifth Avenue and Alder Street.

Nob Hill: The affluent neighborhood from W Burnside Street to NW Pettygrove Street, west of NW Seventeenth Avenue.

NoPo: North Portland.

Nordie's: The Nordstrom department store.

Old Town: The area of downtown north of W Burnside Street and east of NW Broadway. Formerly known as "the North End," "Satan's City," "the Bad Lands," and "the Big Eddy," it was the city's district for prostitution, drugs, and gambling.

The Pearl: The urban district just north of W Burnside Street and west of NW Broadway. A mixed area of expensive condominium lofts and apartments for low-income people. It has the largest concentration of art galleries in the city, as well as restaurants, nightclubs, and small shops. Aka Alimony Flats and Empty-Nest Flats.

Piggott's Folly: The elaborate castle built by Charles H. Piggott in 1892 at 2591 SW Buckingham Avenue and visible on the hillside, south of Portland State University.

Pill Hill: Marquam Hill, just south of downtown Portland, site of several hospitals, including Oregon Health Sciences University (OHSU).

Piss-U: Portland State University, aka Piss-U-Off.

Prosti-tots: Homeless street kids who trade sex for money.

Psycho Safeway: The Safeway supermarket on SW Jefferson Street, between SW Tenth and Eleventh Avenues. Famous for the antics of insane street people, drug-addicted shoplifters, and students from nearby Portland State University.

Pull My Finger: A nickname for *Portlandia,* a huge copper statue by Raymond Kaskey that sits above the entrance to the Portland Building at 1120 SW Fifth Avenue. The statue crouches above the building's front doors and seems to extend its index finger.

Reedies: Students or graduates of Reed College in Southeast Portland, among them Barret Hansen, known now as Dr. Demento.

The Schnitz: The nice, clean, and beige Arlene Schnitzer Concert Hall at SW Broadway and Main

Street, formerly the Paramount, a murky black-and-gold rock concert venue, formerly the Portland movie palace.

The Scum Center: The Rose Festival's "Fun Center" carnival in Tom McCall Waterfront Park.

Silver Dildo: A nickname for the Silverado bar, which features male strippers. See also the Devil's Triangle.

Stinky Town: The nickname for the area below the south end of the St. John's Bridge, site of a derelict plant that used to process natural gas. The plant's crumbling headquarters, topped with a four-sided clock tower, is considered the most photographed landmark in Portland.

String Town: The nickname for the Albina area when it housed Irish, Italian, and German railway workers. Origin unknown.

Sucker Creek Swamp: The original name for Lake Oswego before it was subdivided and marketed as an exclusive bedroom community for the wealthy.

Three Groins in a Fountain: A nickname for the statue *Quest* by Count Alexander von Svoboda on the west side of the Standard Insurance Center, at SW Fifth Avenue and Salmon Street.

Trendy-Third/Trendy-First: NW Twenty-third and Twenty-first Avenues, currently lined with trendy, chic shops and restaurants.

Trustafarians: Slang for would-be hippies and drug, environmental, and anarchy activists who wear hemp and patchouli and pretend to be poor, despite the sizable incomes they receive from trust funds endowed by their wealthy families.

24 Hour Church of Elvis: The art installation and shrine, formerly located at 720 SW Ankeny Street.

Vaseline Flats: The area of Northwest Portland west of the 405 freeway, popular with homosexual men and women, aka "the Swish Alps."

The V-C: The Virginia Café, a bar and restaurant at 725 SW Park Avenue.

The V-Q: The Veritable Quandary, a bar and restaurant at 1220 SW First Avenue.

Willamette: Pronounced "Wil-LAMB-met," from the native word *Wal-lamt,* meaning "spilled water," and referring to the waterfalls south of Portland at Oregon City. Now the name of the river that runs north through Portland.

The Witch House: Either the Simon Benson house (recently restored and moved to the Portland State University campus on the South Park Blocks), or the David Cole mansion at 1441 N McClellan Street, where an old woman used to sit in the tower's cupola watching local kids, or the Stone House, built as a park structure by Italian masons on Balch Creek under the Thurman Street Bridge.

(a postcard from 1981)

Acid and LSD are the same thing. I'm only telling you this because I didn't know it.

This year, I'm nineteen years old and living in a rented room on the second floor at 2221 NW Flanders Street. The Hampton Court Apartments. My friends and I, we buy our jeans at the Squire Shop on SW Broadway and Alder Street. We wear high-waisted, buckle-back carpenter pants with a loop midway down the thigh, so you can hook a hammer there. The Squire Shop has the white-denim painter pants and the striped engineer jeans. We listen to the Flying Lizards and Pink Floyd.

In high school I'd watched a spooky movie called *Focus on Acid*. Acid could make you mistake the gas flame on a stove for a lovely blue carnation. You'd have flashbacks years later and wreck your car.

Still, when some friends suggested eating a tab of LSD and watching the Pink Floyd laser light show at the OMSI (Oregon Museum of Science and Industry) planetarium, I said sure. Let's go.

LSD was lysergic acid diethylamide. A simple alkaloid. Just another chemical. It was science.

This was December, when OMSI used to be in the West Hills, high above the city near the zoo. We sat in the cold parking lot at dusk and each ate a little paper stamp impregnated with LSD, and my friends told me what to expect. First, we'd laugh a lot. We'd smile so long and hard our face muscles would ache for days. Then, we'd grind our teeth. This was important to know so you didn't wear down your molars. My friends talked about how each light and color would bleed a little comet trail. The paint would seem to run down the walls. First, we'd watch the laser light show, then we'd wander through the West Hills mansions and trip on the Christmas lights.

In the OMSI planetarium the seats are in circles around the projector in the center of the round room. My friends sit on one side of me. A woman I don't know sits on my other side. Pink Floyd blares out of speakers and red laser squiggles around the dark, domed ceiling, and I'm laughing so hard I can't stop. They play "Dark Side of the Moon," and my jaws start to ache. They play "The Wall," and the friend on my left side says, "Put something in your mouth." He says, "You're going to wreck your teeth."

He's right, my back teeth feel hot and there's that burned-metal taste you get having a cavity drilled. I'm grinding my teeth that hard.

This is December, so we're wearing denim jackets with fake sheepskin lining. Stocking caps and thick, knitted mufflers. With my muffler stuffed in my mouth, I go back to chewing.

The next thing I know, I'm choking. My throat is full of something soft and dry. I'm gagging, and my mouth is stuffed with something chewy and matted. Some kind of fibers. Or hairs.

In the dark, the laser squiggling and Pink Floyd blasting, my muffler doesn't feel right. It's too soft, and I'm spitting and picking bits of animal fur out of my mouth. If it's mink or rabbit, I don't know, but this is fur.

The woman who sat down next to me, she was wearing a fur coat and dropped it into her seat. She dropped it so one sleeve fell across my lap. That's what I've put in my mouth, and here in the dark, I've chewed, gnawed, gobbled up everything between the elbow and the cuff.

Now my friends are trying to pass me some cleaning solvent poured on a bandanna. To huff. It stinks like dirty socks, and people sitting around us are starting to gripe about the smell.

At any minute the lasers and the music will stop. The lights will come up, and people will get to their feet. They'll slip into their hats and gloves. And the stranger beside me will find a drooly mess where her coat sleeve used to be. Me, I'll be sitting here with wet fur all around my mouth. Strands of fur still stuck between my teeth. Coughing up a mink hair ball.

My friends are elbowing me, still trying to pass me the stinking bandanna soaked in solvent. Carbon tetrachloride, another simple chemical. And the fur coat woman on my other side says, "Christ, what is that smell?"

As the last song ends, before the lights come on, I stand. I tell my friends we're going. Now. I'm shoving them out into the aisle. As the lights come up, I'm climbing over them, telling them, "Run. Don't ask questions, just get outside."

Of course, they think this is a game. So we're running. Outside the fire exit doors, the acres of parking lot are dark, and it's started to snow.

With the snow falling in fat clumps around us, we're running. Through Washington Park at night. Past the zoo and the Christmas lights on the big mansions, each spot of color smearing. Trailing. We're running through the rose garden, the downtown stretched out below. And my friends are laughing. Their fingers and faces stinking of chemical solvent, they run through the falling snow, not thinking this is anything but fun.

Quests: Adventures to Hunt Down

*E*ACH OF THE FOLLOWING is a real trip—minus the risk of flashbacks. Make the effort and live a few hours in somebody else's world. Here are fourteen local outings that prove no way do we all live in the same reality.

1. THE SELF-CLEANING HOUSE

The sign on the gate says DO NOT STEP ON THE POISON IVY OR FEED THE BULL and it's not kidding. That, and the Great Dane, Molly, will rip out your throat.

This is the world-famous Self-Cleaning House, designed and built by Frances Gabe, an artist, an inventor, and a great storyteller. Here in her house the walls are concrete block, with entire walls made of special blocks mortared sideways so the hollow cores form little windows. Sealed on both sides with Plexiglas, the windows hold small knickknacks you never have to dust.

Some open blocks in the wall are glazed with amber glass, giving the rooms a golden honeycomb light. A beehive feeling. "The light ought to go from one side of the house to the other," Frances says, "clear through."

One door is a solid slab of casting resin with slices of bark sealed inside. Frances was so in love with the red-purple color of the local poison oak, she tried to mix paints to match it. She never could, so she tried to save it by casting it inside resin. To her disappointment, the resin turned the bark black.

To clean the house, you just turn on the water to a spinning spray head in the center of each room's ceiling. You add soap through a stint in the plumbing. The wash and rinse water run down the sloped floor and out through the fireplace. You turn on the heat and blower to dry everything. In the kitchen, open work shelves allow all the water to drain through to the floor. A hatch in the wall channels trash down a chute to the garbage can. Clothes are washed and dried as they hang on hangers hooked to a chain that pulls them through each process in a three-part cabinet. The first part is a washing closet, the middle third is a dryer, the last third is the storage closet where the clothes wait, ready to wear.

Frances chose concrete block to dissuade termites, carpenter ants, and gophers. "They're all looking for living quarters and they'd be very happy to share mine with me." Despite the concrete, a chipmunk keeps getting in to eat her bananas.

The walls are covered with paintings and pencil sketches Frances has done, all of them waterproofed to protect them from the overhead soap and water sprays. The floors are sloped a half inch for each ten running feet. The only item that's not waterproof is a rug on the floor that has to be rolled and set aside when the room is washed. The house has withstood two earthquakes, three floods, and the hurricane of the 1962 Columbus Day storm.

Framed on one wall is a U.S. government patent for the Self-Cleaning House. "It was the only patent of its kind the government ever issued," Frances says. "Instead of a single sheet, this is like a *book*." Behind the top sheet there are twenty-five different patents for different aspects of the house.

Today she wears a bright red sweater and slacks, and black-framed glasses. Her gray hair is curly and short. She walks as little as possible, moving from chair to chair, to finally a wheelchair that lets her move around her studio, from her drafting board to her desk to a half dozen other projects. Molly, her Great Dane, is always beside her.

Born Frances Grace Arnholtz in 1915, she went to eighteen different grade schools, moving around with her father, a building contractor. "I was born a most unusual person so I had a heck of a time in school," she says. "Everything moved much too slowly. My last day, I stood up in class and screamed at my teacher, 'You told us that *last* week!'"

She adds, "I just wanted to get an education and get out of there!"

Frances graduated in 1931, at the age of sixteen. At seventeen, she married Herbert Grant Bateson. "He was six-foot-two and I was five-foot-two, and we got kidded a lot," she says. "He was a building contractor, and I was my husband's boss."

After their divorce she changed her last name to Gabe, a name she invented using the first letters of her middle name (Grace) her maiden name (Arnholtz) and her married name (Bateson). She explains, "I added the E to keep it from being 'Gab.'"

The hearth of her bedroom fireplace is paved with hand-cast tiles, printed with her initials, F.G.A.B.

In the 1940s she designed her self-cleaning house and toured the country with a model. It's just returned from a two-year loan to the Women's Museum in Dallas, Texas. "Now," she says, "people are yelling for floor plans for the model."

To see her self-cleaning house, drive south on Interstate 5 through Portland to the Newberg exit. Then take Highway 99W south through Tigard to the town of Newberg. At the far side of the small downtown area, look for the traffic light at Main Street and turn left. Follow Main through another light and a stop sign, where it becomes Dayton Avenue. Follow Dayton Avenue until it crosses a bridge over a ravine. Take the first right turn, onto a gravel road, and veer to the right. The Self-Cleaning House is the last house on this road. But—and I cannot stress this enough—*call first!* The number is 503-538-4946. Be polite and expect to negotiate a small fee for your tour.

Sitting in her studio, with the wide windows looking down into the canyon of Chehalem Creek, Frances Gabe works on more floor plans for her famous house. "In high school," she says, "my psychiatrist told me, 'You're many times over a genius. The world belongs to you, and don't let anyone tell you anything different.'"

2. House of Cunt

Forget the *Vagina Monologues*. This three-woman, two-man theater troupe has gone from parading the street in nothing but G-strings made from human-hair toupees to opening for the Oregon Ballet. Wherever you find them, they'll be pushing the envelope with their experimental comedy and music.

3. Volcano Basketball

On Portland's east side, Mount Tabor, Mount Scott, and Rocky Butte are all volcanic vents left over from the last eruptions of now dormant Mount Hood. Until the next eruption, an asphalt basketball court on Mount Tabor fills the dormant crater.

4. Adult Soapbox Derby

Every August, grown-ups race their homemade cars down the steep slopes of Mount Tabor. Cars crash. People are hurt. And someone wins. It's a blast. Look for the preliminary race around August 10, with the finals two weeks later. Or hang out with the racers at the sponsoring bar, Beulahland, 118 NE Twenty-eighth Avenue. Phone: 503-235-2794.

5. SANTA RAMPAGE

Drinking a hallucinogenic liqueur—made by soaking marijuana in rum, and called "Reindeer Fucker"—the jolly "red tide" of several hundred Santa Clauses crashes elegant holiday parties, storms through swanky restaurants, boogies in strip clubs, and generally keeps Portland's Central Precinct busy and paranoid. Most American cities have their own "Rampage," but Portland's—held the second weekend in December—is still one of the biggest and best. For more details, see "A Postcard from 1996."

6. THE EMILY DICKINSON SING-ALONG

Did you know you can sing any poem by Emily Dickinson to the tune of "The Yellow Rose of Texas"? Well, come the Belle of Amherst's birthday—December 10—join the crowd at Café Lena, 2239 SE Hawthorne Boulevard, to sing the collected works of Dickinson.

7. ABANDONED TIMBERLINE HIGHWAY

From the lower end the old road to Timberline Lodge is almost impossible to find, according to Portland architect Bing Sheldon. The original route to the lodge, it's a curving scenic two-lane road that crosses stone bridges and skirts huckleberry fields. Bing says, "It really is an undiscovered treasure." Like the lodge, the road was built during the Depression but was obsolete and replaced by the end of World War II.

"It's still paved, and you can still drive on it," Bing says. "It's a wonderful engineering feat, built on a six percent grade." To find the old road, he says, start at the top, at Timberline Lodge. Driving down from the lodge, look for the first post of the ski lift and a road that heads off to the right, passing under the ski lift.

8. Fire Department Ride-Alongs

The Portland Fire Bureau responds to about one fire every three hours. If you can wait, you can ride along. According to a spokesman for the bureau, you must be eighteen and, yes, you can ride on the fire engine. The only thing you can't do is go into the fire. Bummer. To make your plans, call the chief at one of the fire stations.

9. That's No Lady

Most people think Gracie Hansen is dead.

Hansen was the queen of Portland for years, the big-busted, loud-laughing queen of the Roaring Twenties Showroom at the Hoyt Hotel, a faux–Gay Nineties palace of antiques and special effects built by some of Hollywood's top set designers.

Before 1961, Gracie Hansen was a schoolteacher from Morton, Washington, who dreamed of chucking the small-town life in central Washington State and moving to Seattle. There, she wanted to stage a burlesque show at the 1962 Seattle World's Fair. "She needed fifty thousand dollars," says choreographer Roxy Leroy Neuhardt. "The story is, she found forty-nine Chinese men with a thousand dollars each and one Greek with a thousand." He says, "And they ended up serving Greek food—for whatever reason."

After the fair closed, the only things to stay were the Space Needle and the Monorail. Harvey Dick, who was renovating Portland's old Hoyt Hotel, recruited Hansen to come south and put on her burlesque show in his new showroom. His bar, the Barbary Coast, had no electricity, only gaslight, and it was famous for the urinals in the men's room: a sculpted, landscaped waterfall you pee into. Says Roxy, "They took a huge dirty old garage and when they were done, you'd swear that whole room had come around the Horn in the last century."

It was at the Hoyt Hotel that local actor Walter Cole first put on a dress. As a lark. It was a gown that Roxy had "borrowed" from Hansen's wardrobe.

"Gracie saw it and she was *very* angry," Walter says. "But she didn't say a word because she didn't know me."

About drag queens, Walter and Roxy say they're nothing new in Portland. Every burlesque and vaudeville program had a female impersonator, usually the master of ceremonies. The famed impersonator Julian Eltinge was a Portland favorite when he toured from New York, and a dozen pictures of him dressed as a woman still hung in Portland's Heilig Theater when it was torn down. Since the early 1900s, the Harbor Club at SW First Avenue and Yamhill Street had offered drag shows. It became the only bar in Oregon declared off-limits to members of the U.S.

Navy. In the 1930s drag shows moved to the Music Hall at 413 SW Tenth Avenue, which became Club Rumba in the 1940s. In the 1950s the *Jewel Box Revue* toured the country with female impersonators from Kansas City and played in Rossini's Clover Room, what's now the office space above the Finnegan's toy store.

In the 1960s Roxy was a choreographer and dancer in Las Vegas. He was in Hollywood when he met Hansen, both of them costume shopping for their respective shows. He came to Portland, but only for sixteen weeks, to help launch the new Roaring Twenties show. One night at the old drag bar Dahl and Penne's, Roxy met Walter Cole, a local actor and businessman. He'd owned Portland's first "Beat" coffeehouse, Café Espresso. And Studio A, a jazz club at SW Second Avenue and Clay Street. He acted at the Firehouse Theater on SW Montgomery Street. "Attorneys and doctors," Walter says, "that's all I ever got to play. At least I didn't have to do my own wardrobe when I wore a suit."

Since the early 1950s, the Imperial Rose Court of Portland had elected an empress every Halloween. In 1974, Pulitzer Prize–winning journalist Randy Shilts was a student at the University of Oregon when he won the national William Randolph Hearst Award for a newspaper article he'd written about the court. But like shanghaiing, brothels, and ghosts, drag queens aren't part of the official Portland history book.

In 1972, wearing Gracie Hansen's gown, using the name Darcelle, Walter Cole became the fifteenth empress of Portland, only the second empress elected in a new city-wide voting system that began the year before.

But Walter didn't just borrow Hansen's gown. He borrowed her entire persona. When the Hoyt Hotel went out of business, Walter in his own way *became* Hansen. Although diabetes took first one leg and then her life, Gracie Hansen lives on, her jokes and dresses and loud personality, in the form of Darcelle XV.

Well, they were sort of Hansen's jokes.

In her act, Walter says, Hansen carried a big feathered fan. But when she was learning a new routine, the fan would be paper so she could write her jokes on the inside. Her memory wasn't so hot. She'd stop, read a joke off the fan, and tell it. "When she needed new material," he says, "she went to see Totie Fields in Las Vegas and smuggled in a *tape recorder.*"

Walter says, "I inherited all her wardrobe, and I'm still using parts of it. Her jewelry. Her sewing room . . . I'm still sewing on some of those sequins and beads and rhinestones from the Hoyt Hotel." He points out a framed photo of himself as the character Darcelle, wearing a sequined blue Gracie Hansen gown.

If you ask, Does it still fit him?

Walter says, "Yes . . . ?"

And the staff of his nightclub laughs.

"Okay!" he says. "So I added some feathers on the side. That's no sin!"

In 1972, when Walter opened his nightclub in Old Town, Roxy was in the original show. His first night tap dancing there, "Roxy's first *boy* tap dance got this," Walter says and claps once. "The next night, in drag, he got a standing ovation because nobody'd ever seen a tap-dancing drag queen."

Officially called "Walter Cole Presents: That's No Lady—That's Darcelle XV and Company," Walter and Roxy still run the last real burlesque show in town. In the North End's dark tradition of cabarets and music halls, it's a storefront theater, where—sick or well—the show must go on. Even now, at seventy-one years old, Walter Cole still adjusts the stage lights. He cleans the toilets. He makes his own costumes. When it rains too hard, the gutters flood the basement, and mopping up is also his job.

But when the curtain rises, he's wearing Gracie Hansen's gowns and jewelry, laughing her laugh. Telling her jokes. Well . . . telling Totie Fields's jokes.

"The only way I'll retire is when they plant me," Walter says. "And I hope it's during a full house."

"And he's just gotten a laugh," Roxy says.

"And I've just gotten a standing ovation," Walter says.

Darcelle's is at 208 NW Third Avenue. Phone: 503-222-5338.

10. BEHIND CLOSED DOORS

Portland is chockablock with beautiful, historic houses, and on the right day, you can walk right in the front door. To qualify for property tax breaks, the owners of historic houses and buildings must open them to the public at least one day each year. On any day you can go to the website of the State Historic Preservation Office, www.shpo.state.or.us, and find out which local houses are open.

11. Monk-for-a-Month

Here's getting away from it *all*. Live as a Trappist monk for thirty days at the Our Lady of Guadalupe Trappist Abbey. You'll be out of bed for vigil prayers at 4:15 every morning and spend your days working with fellow monks, binding books, baking fruitcakes, and tending the forest that surrounds their isolated abbey. You'll be assigned a mentor to show you the ropes. The monastery is southwest of Portland, in the small town of Lafayette. Phone: 503-852-0107. Or write: Monastic Life Retreat, Trappist Abbey, Lafayette, OR 97127.

12. Triceratops Cleaning

Sixty-five million years ago, a baby triceratops was trying to cross a river in what would someday be eastern Wyoming. Well, the little tyke didn't make it. She drowned. Now she's "field jacketed" in thick plaster and waiting for you to come help scrape away the millennia of hardened mud. According to Greg Dardis, OMSI earth science lead educator, this cleaning will take the next fifteen to twenty years.

"Paleontology is all about humility and patience," Greg says. .

"And *calluses*," adds volunteer Art Johnstone, as he scrapes away with a dental pick. The Oregon Museum of Science and Industry is at 1945 SE Water Avenue.

13. EVICTION COURT

For anyone who thinks the tradition of oral storytelling is dead, this is a must-see. Go to the Multnomah County Courthouse, downtown, at SW Fourth Avenue and Main Street. Enter through the main door on SW Fourth Avenue and go to Room 120. Eviction Court meets Monday through Friday at 9:00 A.M., and all dirty laundry is loudly thrown around. It is the professional wrestling of the courthouse.

14. THE DE-VIRGINIZING DANCE

The *Rocky Horror Picture Show* has been playing as a midnight movie at the Clinton Street Theater for more than twenty years. According to Rachel, a student at the Metropolitan Learning Center in Northwest Portland, anyone who has never been to the costumed audience-participation event is labeled a "virgin" and hauled up onstage for a rite of passage. The legally eighteen are separated from the under-eighteen, and . . . "They took this one girl up onstage and stripped her naked," Rachel says. "Then they wrapped her in gauze and dribbled this sticky red stuff on her and called her a used tampon." Rachel calls this "the de-virginizing dance." After all that you must swear to come see the show at least three times a year.

The *Rocky Horror Picture Show* plays every Saturday night at the Clinton Street Theater, 2522 SE Clinton Street.

(a postcard from 1985)

Our third night shooting on location, no one can find our meat.

The set dressers and props people are pissed. They bought special cuts of meat for this, steaks thick as dictionaries. Chops big around as tennis shoes. They spent time rubbing the raw meat with face powder so it wouldn't shine under the hot lights. So it would look okay on camera.

This is a music video being shot at Corno's Supermarket at SE Union Avenue and Morrison Street. The band is called Cavalcade of Stars, sometimes just COS, and the song is called "Butcher Boy." All night, from the time the market closes until it opens, a video crew is here on location. Night after night.

The chorus boys are dressed as butchers in long white coats, but with big blue-eye shadow eyes and cheekbones defined with smears of plum and magenta. Their hair, moussed and teased into stiff crowns. The chorus girls wear oversized sweatshirts in Day-Glo yellow or pink, with the collar and sleeves ripped off. They wear striped tights and pull the sweatshirts to one side so one bare shoulder always shows. Their hair is streaked with bright green or pink and tied with scraps of orange or blue lace. Their eyes are sunk into deep holes surrounded with black mascara.

For take after take the boys flop the steaks around behind the butcher counter, trying to look busy, tossing the meat with dirty hands and dropping it on the floor. The girls dance with shopping carts as partners.

Local celebrities make cameo appearances. The rock critic John Wendeborn drinks champagne in the background of one shot. Billy Rancher, the lead singer of Billy Rancher and the

Unreal Gods, looks thin and cool, his hair frosted in streaks, his band poised to be Portland's next Quarterflash.

Me, one night out bar hopping with friends, a stranger gave me a business card and said to come for an audition. Now my role is to give the lead singer, Rhonda Kennedy, a come-hither look and make love to her in the meat locker. While dry ice fog cascades over us, we writhe naked in an antique bed surrounded by frozen sides of beef.

The blue and red lights in the meat locker are melting the frozen meat. Pork and beef blood drips on us. It drips on the purple satin bedsheets. Rhonda gives me my first cocaine, a fat envelope I take into a bathroom stall. I have no idea what to do, so I poke my nose into the white dust and inhale it all in one long breath. My face flushed red, dusted with white, I could be a slab of our missing meat.

And Rhonda says, "That was for *all of us.*"

She and I, we embrace and spin together under the colored lights, we fall into the big damp bed, and Rhonda's breasts bounce out the top of her black lace negligee.

And the director yells, "Cut."

Between takes, while the crew sets up the lights and cameras for the next shot, Billy Rancher and the chorus girls link arms and walk down SE Union Avenue, filling the empty street at three or four in the morning. These flashy, glam kids, they walk the half block to the all-night Burns Brothers truck stop. They smoke clove cigarettes and order coffee and dazzle the tired gas jockeys.

Almost no one here is getting paid. We're each promised a percent of the profits from the sale of the video. We pray for a heavy rotation on MTV.

Within a couple of years, Billy Rancher will be dead from cancer. John Wendeborn will be fired. The Corno's Supermarket will close. Union Avenue will be renamed for Martin Luther King Jr. Even the greasy old Burns Brothers truck stop will be replaced with a new minimart.

Soon enough, the Dalai Lama will slap Rhonda Kennedy across the face and she'll become a force for the liberation of Tibet. She'll chaperone a team of Buddhist monk "skeleton dancers" on the Lollapalooza Tour with the Beastie Boys. Fifteen years after we spent our night in a bed soaked with cold animal blood, Rhonda tells me nothing is as nasty as sharing a tour bus bathroom with Buddhist monks: They're not allowed to touch their penises and refuse to piss sitting down.

Still, that night wearing all our blue eye shadow, we're thinking this will make us famous. We will look young and hip—forever.

It's at some point that night the set dressers get word about the missing meat. The extra-thick steaks and chops, coated with makeup, fingerprints, and floor dirt, was ground into hamburger. By mistake, the day shift sold it all to customers.

Chow: Eating Out

Now that you've read the preceding story about dirty meat . . . let's go straight into planning dinner. Some of my favorite cooks have agreed to sacrifice their secret recipes here. Make one, or make them all, and have a best-of-Portland dinner party. If you're in town eating at any of the following places, chances are I'm at the next table.

THE ALIBI

With sculpted hula dancers under black light, woven palm fronds and coconuts, this is Portland's answer to *Gilligan's Island*. Portland's only tiki bar, the Alibi is at 4024 N Interstate Avenue. Phone: 503-287-5335. It's the summertime home of "Exotiki," the annual festival of bad tropical music, featuring twenty-four-hour pagan voodoo weddings. Wintertime, it's the stomping grounds for the Santa Rampage karaoke singers.

DELTA CAFÉ

According to café owner Anastasia Corya, these fritters make a great appetizer. According to cook and filmmaker Ryan Rothermel—whose films include *Ampersand* and *Lover or Liver*—you might add two diced jalapeño peppers to the dip. These recipes are for restaurant quantities, so throw a party or do the math to cut them down. Better yet, go to the Delta Café at 4607 SE Woodstock Boulevard. There isn't a disappointment on the whole menu. Phone: 503-771-3101.

FRITTERS

12 cups white flour
4 teaspoons baking powder
2 teaspoons salt
12 eggs
5 cups milk
¾ pound butter, melted
4 cups corn kernels, raw
4 cups cooked black-eyed peas (see recipe below)

Mix the dry ingredients. Add the remaining ingredients and mix well. Heat an inch of vegetable oil in a frying pan and cook the fritters until golden brown.

FRITTER DIP

5 pounds cooked black-eyed peas (8 cups)
1 27-ounce can diced green chiles
1 pound jack cheese (4 cups), grated
½ pound butter, melted

Mix all the ingredients together. Put one-third in a food processor and blend it into a paste. Mix the paste back into the remaining two-thirds. Heat in a double boiler until the cheese is melted and smooth.

BLACK-EYED PEAS

10 pounds dry black-eyed peas
1 bunch celery, chopped
2 yellow onions, chopped
4 carrots, sliced
4 tablespoons salt
2 tablespoons black pepper
2 bay leaves
¼ pound whole garlic cloves (about 1 cup), peeled

Put all ingredients in a stockpot and boil 45 minutes or until tender. Add water if needed.

FULLER'S RESTAURANT

Come have breakfast or lunch with the locals, but don't leave without a loaf of Fuller's incredible fresh-baked bread. It's at 136 NW Ninth Avenue. Phone: 503-222-5608.

LE HAPPY

Owner John Brodie also manages the band Pink Martini, a popular band here in the States but cult heroes in France. "When I've traveled with Pink Martini in the U.S. and France," John says, "we always seemed to find a good creperie. So I decided to open one here. So now when the French visit us, we can take them to an authentic creperie in Portland, Oregon." Wherever you are, check out the website www.lehappy.com. The restaurant is at 1011 NW Sixteenth Avenue. Phone: 503-226-1258.

LE HAPPY'S FAUX VEGAN CREPES

Traditionally, crepes are served folded over in a half circle, or with the sides of the round crepe folded in to make a perfect square. To make at home, we've adapted this recipe to serve smaller rolled crepes.

Makes 8 crepes, 4 servings

BUCKWHEAT CREPE BATTER
¾ cup all-purpose flour
¼ cup buckwheat flour
1⅓ cup whole milk
2 eggs
¼ cup water
¼ teaspoon salt
Pepper to taste
2 teaspoons butter, melted
Vegetable oil for frying

MUSHROOM RAGOUT

1 pound mushrooms (about 6 cups), chopped

2 tablespoons butter

1½ teaspoons porcini powder (see note)

½ cup dry sherry

Salt and pepper to taste

1 cup heavy cream

8 tablespoons Gruyère cheese (or Swiss), grated

2 cups fresh spinach, chopped

4 ounces mild goat cheese (½ cup)

2 tablespoons fresh parsley, chopped

½ teaspoon fresh thyme, minced

4 tablespoons crème fraîche (see note)

TO MAKE CREPES: Whisk together the white and buck-wheat flour. Add the milk and eggs and stir to combine. Add the water, salt, pepper, and melted butter and stir until smooth. The batter should be the consistency of heavy cream.

Heat an 8-inch nonstick crepe pan (or omelet pan) over medium-high heat and brush lightly with vegetable oil. Pour ¼ cup batter into the hot pan and quickly tip and swirl to evenly coat the pan. Cook, over medium-high heat, until the bottom is golden brown. Flip and cook second side briefly. Remove to a warm plate. Repeat with remaining batter. Hold crepes in a warm oven until needed.

TO MAKE MUSHROOM RAGOUT: Sauté the mush-rooms in the butter over medium-high heat until the mushrooms are tender and beginning to give up some of their liquid. Stir in the porcini powder and dry sherry and cook over high heat until the sherry is almost completely evaporated. Season with salt and pepper and stir in the cream. Cook over high heat until the cream is reduced and the sauce is thick. Taste and season again with salt and pepper if necessary. Keep warm until ready to fill crepes.

TO ASSEMBLE CREPES: Preheat oven to 250 degrees. Place a warm crepe on a plate and sprinkle with 1 tablespoon Gruyère. Top with ¼ cup chopped spinach and one-eighth of the mushroom ragout. Crumble 1 tablespoon goat cheese over the mushrooms, and sprinkle with a mixture of parsley and thyme. Roll the crepe around the filling and arrange seamside down on a baking dish. Fill and roll remaining crepes and place in baking pan. Cover and bake for 10 to 15 minutes or until crepes are heated through. Drizzle with crème fraîche and serve hot.

Note: Dried porcini mushrooms are available at specialty markets. To make porcini powder, pulverize dried mushrooms in a spice grinder or blender.

Crème fraîche is two parts heavy cream to one part buttermilk (blend, let stand overnight until thick, then refrigerate).

WESTERN CULINARY INSTITUTE

Portland's old guard of rich cheapskates don't want you to know this little secret of theirs. The waiters and chefs at the institute have not just their jobs and wages riding on your satisfaction, but their grades and future as well. The dining room is swank and intimate, and the service is very snappy with no more than two tables per server. Fat's no issue—it's real butter and cream—and the food's terrific. All this and free parking. It's no wonder folks flock down from the West Hills for fine dining at a fast-food price.

The dining room is at 1316 SW Thirteenth Avenue. Phone: 503-294-9770. Lunch is served 11:30–1:00, five courses for $9.95. Dinner is served 6:00–8:00, six courses for $19.95. Thursday is buffet night, offering at least thirty-five items. *Very important:* Reservations are recommended at least a week in advance.

WILD ABANDON

The building is a former link in the chain of Ginger's Sexy Saunas—several massage parlor "jack shacks" that used to dot Portland in the 1970s. You can't get a handjob here, but you can get a great dinner, and breakfast on the weekend. Say hello to the owner, Michael Cox, and look for the actress Linda Blair, a vegan regular. The restaurant is at 2411 SE Belmont Street. Phone: 503-232-4458.

The menu changes, but I always look for these:

DEAN BLAIR'S LEMON-LAVENDER SCONES

1½ cups flour
½ tablespoon baking powder
½ teaspoon baking soda
½ cup brown sugar
½ teaspoon salt

¼ pound cold unsalted butter, cubed
1 tablespoon lavender flowers
Zest from one lemon
½ cup buttermilk
1 small egg
1 teaspoon vanilla extract

Preheat the oven to 350 degrees.

In a medium bowl sift together the flour, baking powder, baking soda, sugar, and salt. Add the cubed butter, lavender, and lemon zest. In a separate bowl combine the buttermilk, egg, and vanilla and whip with a fork. Create a well in the center of the dry ingredients and pour in the buttermilk mixture. Combine with a rubber spatula until just moistened. Transfer to a cookie sheet and form the dough into a wheel roughly 9 inches in diameter and ¾ inch thick. Score it into eight pie slices and top with brown sugar. Bake for about 25 to 30 minutes.

(a **postcard** from 1986)

Somewhere a man's hollering about devils and demons. From some other hospital room he's bellowing and screaming about how the niggers and fags are out to get him. You can hear him all over the third floor when he screams, "Get away from me, you cunt!" And his shouting just goes on and on.

This is Emanuel Hospital, the big medical complex at the east end of the Fremont Bridge. I'm here as a volunteer for a charity hospice. My job is to take people places, mostly relatives of dying people. Mostly, I drive visiting mothers from their motel to the hospital. After their son or daughter is dead, I might drive them to the airport for their flight home.

Today we're waiting for a man to die of AIDS while his mother sits beside his bed, holding his hand and singing "Twinkle, Twinkle Little Star," again and again. It was his favorite song when he was a boy, she says. Now he's just bones and body hair, curled on his side under a thin knit blanket. A pump injects him with morphine every few seconds. His face has the slack look, yellow and dried, that means this is our last trip to the hospital.

The Mom is from Minnesota—I think. Maybe Montana. It's been my experience that nobody dies like in the movies. No matter how sick they look, they're waiting for you to leave. Around midnight, when I finally take his mom back to her Travelodge on E Burnside Street, when he's all alone, then her son will die.

For now she sings "Twinkle, Twinkle Little Star," over and over until it doesn't make any sense. Until the words turn into a mantra. A bird's song. Just sounds without meaning. I look at my watch.

It's then the yelling starts. The rant about spics and niggers and fags and cunts. It's a man's voice, huge and hoarse, shouting from some room nearby.

A nurse comes into the room to explain. The shouting man has taken a drug overdose, they really can't sedate him because they have no idea what drugs he's already taken. The nurse says the man's in restraints, down the hall, but we're all going to have to tolerate his shouting until he wears himself out.

Still, the man's shouting about gooks and kikes.

With each shout the dying son jerks a little, winces, and his mother stops singing. After a little while, a few automatic injections of morphine, the man's still shouting about demons and devils, and the Mom picks up her purse. She gets to her feet.

She goes to the door, and I follow.

She's giving up, I figure, heading back to the motel. To the airport. To Minnesota.

As we're going down the hospital hallway, the yelling gets louder, closer, until we're right outside the man's room. The door's half open, and inside is a curtain pulled shut around a hospital bed. The Mom goes in. She goes through the slit in the curtain.

The man's shouting, calling her a cunt. Telling her to get out.

I go to look, and the man's naked in bed, his hands and ankles buckled to the chrome bed rails with leather straps. He's huge, filling the whole mattress, and wrestles against the leather straps until every muscle pops up, huge with blood and veins, smooth with tattoos of snakes and women in bright red and blue. His face flush, he yells for the "fucking" nurse. She should "fucking get in here." His hands and ankles strapped down, he twists and fights. The way a fish arches and flops on hot sand. The inside of each arm is poked with IV needles. The skin scabbed from old injections.

The Mom sets her purse on the edge of his mattress. She says, "What pretty tattoos."

I remember that because it's the only thing she said. Then she takes a tissue out of her purse, an old, crumpled tissue.

You can't tell anyone about a naked man without getting to his penis and balls. They're the only part of him not fighting. And not covered with tattoos. His genitals are just red, wadded flesh in the nest of his black pubic hair.

At this point, I've been volunteering around hospitals since I was fourteen. Where I grew up, you had to perform several hundred hours of volunteer work to be confirmed in the Catholic Church. About the only place to do this was Our Lady of Lourdes Hospital. Fourteen years old and I was cleaning delivery rooms. No rubber gloves, and I'm tossing out afterbirths. Washing coagulated blood out of stainless steel pans, I loved it. My other job in the hospital was dusting shelves in the pharmacy. A few years down the road and this would've been my dream job—me alone with this smorgasbord of painkillers—but for now, it was beyond boring.

Me, I thought I'd seen everything.

Here and now, the Mom uses the tissue from her purse to lift the man's limp penis. It's about the size of a boneless thumb. She lifts it straight up and lets it flop back down. The man's balls are cupped between his hairy thighs. He squirms to get away from her, but he can't.

Both of us standing inside the closed curtain, I don't stop her. My job is just to drive her around. And wait. I look at my watch, again.

The man's red-faced and shouting about the fucking devils. The demons are touching him. He's screaming for help.

The Mom, her hand puts the tissue back into her purse. And when her hand comes out, it's holding a baby pin.

The man's screaming. He's screaming, "Fuck. Cunt. Nigger. Fag."

Again and again until it doesn't make any sense. Until the words turn into a mantra. A bird's song. Just sounds without meaning. I look at my watch.

And the Mom clicks the pin open.

The door to the room is half closed. It's hospital policy not to close the door to a patient's room all the way. Everyone on the third floor can hear the man, but no one's listening.

The Mom drives the needle into the man's thigh.

She sticks the needle in, and the man bellows. He squeals until his screams break into sobs. She stabs again, and he's sobbing and begging her to stop. He's sobbing until he's quiet.

By then I'm standing at the edge of the bed. I'm leaning in, holding my breath. We don't know this yet, but in that other room the mother's son is already dead.

Haunts: Where to Rub Elbows with the Dead

*F*ROM GHOST STORIES to cold spots, the dead seem to linger among the living in Portland. Here are sixteen local opportunities to look up old friends.

1. NORTHWEST PARANORMAL INVESTIGATIONS

Bob and Renee Chamberlain have been bitten, spit on, bruised, and flipped off—all by ghosts.

As the founders of Northwest Paranormal Investigations, that's just part of their job while videotaping and audio recording, documenting and protecting the spirits and cemeteries around the Portland area.

"Ten years ago," Bob says, "we'd never given the paranormal a second thought—*never.*" Back then, they'd just built a new house and cared for Renee's mother as she died of cancer. But after she died, they'd still hear her cough in the house. They'd hear the dead woman stacking pans in the kitchen. They'd smell her cigarettes. Lights started turning on and off. Their pit bull, Titan, would sit, staring at her photo on the wall.

"We're sane people," Renee says. "But at first I didn't think I was. I thought I was just grieving over my mom."

The toilet tissue would unroll in a heap on the floor. The toilet lid would slam shut, and the toilet would flush. A small statue of a rocking horse would move around the living room. Their two kids heard it all, but no one in the family mentioned it to each other until Renee met with two visiting writers, in town on a book tour, who specialized in the paranormal.

Now they know the difference between a "partial apparition" and a "full apparition." They've put together a group of ghost hunters with chapters in Portland, Saint Helens, and Oregon City. They spend their evenings in places like the Klondike, a haunted hotel and restaurant in downtown Saint Helens, where Bob videotaped a stream of flying "spirit orbs," glowing balls of light that hover and veer down the hallways and around the camera like a "glowing school of fish." On a recent trip they led a film crew from the Fox network to the site of Wellington, Washington, where the whole town was wiped out in a 1920s landslide. There, spirit orbs are visible to the naked eye, and a woman's voice calls to you in broad daylight.

"They came out of there blubbering idiots," Bob says. "They were so in awe."

Bob is a big man, handsome with a square jaw. Renee is pretty, with blond hair piled on her head. Locally, they've found proof of hauntings at the Pittock Mansion in Portland's West Hills. The John McLoughlin House in Oregon City. And in the downtown tunnel system. The Little Church in Sellwood, near the entrance to Oakes Amusement Park, has a "steady flow of orbs going inside every evening," according to Bob. Renee and Bob say that something very basic about the Portland area, something organic, possibly the soil, allows spirits to manifest there more easily.

Before joining the Chamberlains for a meeting or outing with Northwest Paranormal Investigations, here are a few things to know:

"Spirits are always here for a reason," Bob says. "Either they have unfinished business. Or they don't know they're dead. Or they're pranksters."

He adds, "Those spirits feed off of you. If you're an angry person, that's what you'll get. If you're happy-go-lucky, you'll get that."

The more open-minded you are, the more emotionally sensitive, the more you'll experience. Spirit activity is more likely during a full or new moon, or two to three days before an electrical storm.

Membership dues are $2.50 per month, and the Chamberlains hate the term *ghostbusters*. To contact them, go to www.northwestparanormal.freehomepage.com.

"We meet more people who believe than skeptics," Bob says, "but even the most intelligent people have seen things they can't explain."

The group also locates and maintains historic cemeteries and patrols them on Halloween to prevent vandalism.

Before Renee's mother died, Bob had become so obsessed about death that he couldn't sleep. Now that fear is gone, for the whole family. "There's something out there other than just dying and staying where you're put," he says. "It may sound morbid, but I actually look forward to what I'll see on the other side."

The Chamberlains have moved several times, but Renee's mother is still with them. "People think spiritual entities are confined to one area," Renee says, "but they're wrong."

Now, when the rocking horse statue moves, Renee just moves it back, saying, "Mom, I like the rocking horse *right here*. Now, don't move it again!"

2. THE PORTLAND MEMORIAL

It looks like an apartment building rising above SE Bybee Street, just before Bybee curves to merge with SE Thirteenth Avenue. A combination of towering and sprawling wings, built in Victorian, Art Deco, and Spanish styles, it houses more than 58,000 residents with room for another 120,000. It's a 3.5-acre city within the city. A city of the dead.

Started in 1901, the Portland Memorial has expanded into a chilly, carpeted maze of marble, concrete, bronze, and brass. You'll find Tiffany stained-glass windows, Carrara marble statues and fountains. Overstuffed sofas and chairs sit in little groupings. Stairways wind up and down. The long vaults link together to make vistas that seem to stretch forever.

Within ten minutes you'll be confused and lost. After fifteen minutes you'll panic. But while you're hunting for the way out, look for the crypt of Mayo Methot, Humphrey Bogart's first wife. After she died in 1951, a dozen roses arrived here every week for decades. Also, look for the Rae Room, the memorial's biggest crypt. Lined with stained glass, the vault holds two freestanding sarcophaguses and is opened only one day each year. The story is, George Rae married his maid, Elizabeth, twenty-six years his junior, so no family members will visit except on Memorial Day.

And, yes, this is the mausoleum I used as the basis for my second novel, *Survivor*. Part of the book I even wrote here, but the air is freezing and your fingers get stiff, fast. The Portland Cacophony Society (portland.cacophony.org) occasionally hosts outings to explore the labyrinth. On a rainy day it's a good place to walk, tracing the history of Portland's pioneer families. Or maybe just sit and read a spooky book, surrounded by the dead, in a huge window that looks over the black swamp of Oakes Bottom, toward the spinning colored lights of the amusement park.

The Portland Memorial is at SE Fourteenth Avenue and Bybee Street. For hours, call 503-236-4141.

3. MOUNT GLEALL CASTLE

In 1892 pioneer Charles H. Piggott set out to build a castle "in which no two rooms would be alike and in which there would be no angles or straight lines." To name it, he combined the first two letters of each of his children's first names: Gladys, Earl, and Lloyd. Using bricks from the brickyard he owned on Sandy Boulevard, he built his castle at 2591 SW Buckingham Avenue, on the hillside south of Portland State University. A year later, in 1893, Piggott lost his fortune and had to sell his dream home.

In the hundred-plus years since then, the castle has had almost as many residents. In the 1960s it was available as a fantasy rental, and Portland natives say the Grateful Dead crashed there long enough to give Piggott's castle the nickname "the Dead Castle." People also say Piggott's ghost has never left the turreted, brick castle, now painted white, with a sauna installed in the tower.

One explanation is the system of tin tubes that Piggott installed as an intercom system throughout the house. Supposedly, the system picks up noise from downtown and voices from far rooms, amplifies them, and carries them around the house. The intercom was removed in the 1920s, but the reports of strange noises and voices continue.

4. Hoodoo Antiques

Nobody was more surprised than Mike Eadie, owner of Hoodoo Antiques, when people told him that a woman was lurking inside his shop late at night. When it was closed and locked, the alarms were set, and Mike was home with his wife, you could look in through the big display windows and see a woman in a long dress and a bonnet standing near the back of the shop.

Years ago, Eadie's mother-in-law, Ellen Wellborn, had an artist's studio in the Erickson's Saloon building nearby, once a major combination of gambling hall, beer parlor, and whorehouse, boasting the longest bar in the world. In what was once a prostitute's crib, Ellen found a lovely pencil portrait tucked between the clapboards of the wall. The picture is oval, about six by four inches, and shows a young woman wearing a bonnet and a typical 1860s dark dress.

Ellen gave it to Mike, who's hung the small picture in his store, just inside the front door, but not so you can see it from the street. Even inside, unless you know where to look, you'd never notice it.

Since then, night after night, walking tours pass the shop and see someone inside. They insist she's not a reflection, the woman in a long dress and bonnet, standing in the shadows near the back of the store. Still, the motion detectors don't trip. And nothing is ever taken.

Hoodoo Antiques is at 122 NW Couch Street.

5. BAGDAD THEATER

There are parts of the Bagdad Theater at 3702 SE Hawthorne Boulevard that the employees just don't go into.

Built by Universal Studios as a movie palace in 1927, the theater offered live vaudeville acts until the 1940s. Today it's a combination beer pub and movie theater. Behind the huge movie screen is a separate theater, closed since the 1970s, that may someday become condominiums and a rooftop bar. But right now, it's supposed to be haunted by the ghost of a movie projectionist who hanged himself behind the screen on Christmas Eve decades ago.

That story is decades old. Whenever the auditorium's cantankerous lighting system acts up, they've always blamed the suicide.

According to theater manager Jason McEllrath, someone hung a cardiopulmonary resuscitation dummy behind the screen. They hung it years ago, and the dusty, spooky thing still dangles back there, ready to scare the uninitiated.

The theater basements are another story. The front one, along SE Hawthorne, is pretty ordinary. However, the back basements under the stage and backstage . . . "That's just plain scary," Jason says. "There's no lights, and it's full of creepy junk. Doors that go nowhere. We just don't go down there."

Besides the unexplained lights flickering off and on, employees also report cold spots and chilly drafts in rooms with no ventilation.

6. North Portland Library

A few years ago, this former Carnegie library at 512 N Killingsworth Street was renovated and security cameras were installed throughout. Every few seconds the view from a different one of the cameras appears on the video monitor behind the front desk. Soon after renovation, librarians watching the monitor saw an old man seated alone in the enormous second-floor meeting hall. The image only appears for a few seconds before the system cycles to the view from the next camera, but it shows enough to panic the staff. Still, every time they stampede upstairs to find the trespasser, they find the meeting room locked and empty.

Supposedly, the camera still shows the old man upstairs, but only occasionally, despite an increased effort to keep the room locked.

7. CATHEDRAL PARK

This park gets its name from the towering gothic arches that carry the Saint John's Bridge overhead. These arches march through the park, creating a sort-of cathedral effect. It's a wide-open park of lawns and play equipment, but not long ago it was a wasteland of briar thickets and hobo jungles, warehouses, and old wharves.

For most of the twentieth century local kids earned summer money by picking strawberries, raspberries, and boysenberries on outlying farms. These kids would wait, early in the morning, on street corners where the "Berry Buses" would pick them up. The buses took them to work and brought them home.

In the 1930s a young girl was kidnapped while waiting for the Berry Bus in North Portland. According to local legend, she was taken to the bushes below the north end of the Saint John's Bridge, tortured, and killed. Even now that Cathedral Park is a nice garden and hosts a summer jazz festival, nearby residents say you can still hear that one girl screaming in the park on warm summer nights.

8. SAUVIE ISLAND

Once called Wappato Island, this island between the Columbia River, the Willamette River, and the Multnomah Channel was home to a village of some fifty thousand members of the Multnomah tribe. Even before Portland was founded, smallpox brought by early explorers had left the island a deserted ruin of rotting huts and scarred survivors.

Today you can still find arrowheads scattered along the Columbia River beaches. Early morning joggers and late-evening walkers also report almost identical encounters with a naked Multnomah youth. The adolescent boy walks along the waterline and doesn't seem aware of anything except the river and the sand.

More recently, so many cremated nudists have been spread on "clothing optional" Collins Beach that most level areas above the tide line are layered in the telltale crunchy white grit of crushed bone.

9. Heathman Hotel's Haunted Photograph

At first glance the photograph looks ordinary. It shows the wood-paneled Tea Court of the Heathman Hotel at 1001 SW Broadway. There are paintings by Andy Warhol. A crystal chandelier from the American embassy in Czecho-slovakia. A big, blazing fireplace. Flowers, plants, chairs, and sofas. There's the grand piano where Sting and Wynton Marsalis and Arlo Guthrie sit and play for hours when they stay here.

In the photograph it's September 21, 2001, and the hotel's previous owners are officially passing the keys to the new owners. Near the fireplace, just outside the circle of people, a soft, glowing figure stands beside a chair. It's nothing you'd notice at first, but it's there.

"A guy took this picture," says Jeff Jobe, the hotel's general manager, "and the ghost was there. We've tried to reason it away, but we can't. Those lamps in the photo only have thirty-watt bulbs in them."

Charles Barkley stays here, signing his name "Billy Crystal." Billy Crystal stays here, signing as "Charles Barkley." For satirist David Sedaris, the Heathman is a second home, the only place he'd want to live in the United States outside of New York City. Jeff says, "At some point in the history of the hotel, this became *the* place for authors to stay. It's just the buzz." In fact so many famous writers stay here, the hotel's library has collected some three thousand signed first editions.

It's easy to see why guests keep coming back and why some guests have never left.

Larry Adams, the hotel's director of operations, can tell you the maids are a little squeamish about cleaning Rooms 803 and 703. If a guest is going to complain, chances are they're booked in 803 or one of the rooms directly below it. People return to 803 or 703 to find the bottles of water half drunk. Desks are moved. Beds are mussed. Towels used. Cups and glasses are turned over. The television is turned on or a chair is moved. Of course, they complain.

But when Larry or Jeff check the key card system, it shows no one has entered the room since the last time the guest left. "There's no way to fudge the system," Jeff says. "You just *can't* get in."

In September 1999, the psychic Char, author of *Questions from Earth, Answers from Heaven,* stayed in Room 703. Another psychic, Echo Bodiene, stayed in the room for a week to dialogue with the spirit. The two women agree it's the spirit of a man who jumped from Room 803, committing suicide and now haunting each room he looked into on his way down.

Larry says the man was scarred or deformed in some way. "People made fun of the way he looked, and he was tired of it," he says, adding the suicide took place not long after the hotel opened in 1927.

In 1975 a blind guest named Harris killed himself in Room 303. His body was found by housekeeper Fidel Semper, now retired from the hotel. Employees and guests also report cold spots in the hallways, phantoms breezing past them, and the sound of footsteps on the grand staircase when it's empty.

Now when a guest complains, Jeff shows them the key card records, saying, "Look. Here's the readout. Nothing was stolen. He only moves furniture." Assuring them, "He doesn't make noise. He only drinks the water."

10. Lydia

A ghost named Lydia is supposed to haunt the Pied Cow Coffeehouse, a Victorian mansion at 3244 SE Belmont Street. The restaurant that occupied the space previously,

Butter Toes, is supposed to have also been host to Lydia's presence.

11. THE HAUNTED BATHROOMS

In the bathrooms the trash lids start to swing by themselves. Water will start running in the bathroom sinks. You'll hear the sounds of someone doing their business in empty toilet stalls. Some mornings, the staff will arrive early to find the water running in sinks. Some nights, they'll hear the noise of parties in the private upstairs dining rooms that are empty.

At the Rose and Raindrop Restaurant, server Jenna Hill says, "A lot of people will go into the bathroom late at night and come out looking kind of pale."

Built by Edward Holman in 1880, the building at 532 SE Grand Avenue was for years the Barber and Hill Undertakers and Embalmers. In the dozen apartments above the restaurant, it's a given that clocks will reset themselves all the time. Mark Roe, an artist who sells his work at Portland's Saturday Market, remembers, "I had a girlfriend who lived in an apartment above the restaurant, and I'd stay overnight. You could *still* smell the formaldehyde coming up through the floors."

The building once housed the Nickelodeon Theater, one of Portland's first vaudeville and silent movie houses, as well as Ralph's Good Used Furniture store, owned by Ralph Jacobson, the man who taught the Hippo Hardware team their trade.

It was designed by Justus F. Krumbein, who also designed the original state capitol building. For several years it housed a restaurant called Digger O'Dells, named for the gravedigger character from the *Life of Riley* radio show in the 1940s.

The two private dining rooms—where you can hear mysterious parties at night—are named the Duffy and Baker rooms, after two traveling vaudeville troupes. Both rooms are directly over the haunted bathrooms. These, Jenna Hill says, are above the crematory ovens in the basement. Those ovens are walled over, she says, but still there.

12. UNMARKED GRAVES

Nobody wanted to work late nights at Michaels (the arts and crafts store) when it was located at NE 122nd and Sandy Boulevard. Lights and a loud compressor would turn themselves off and on at night. It seems that road widening has crowded the adjacent pioneer cemetery, and scores of graves have been misplaced. The rumor among Michaels employees is that their old parking lot is paving over a good share of those plots. As a result several lawsuits against the county are pending.

Several employees at the neighboring Kmart confirm these stories, mostly the lights and noise at night, but asked not to be identified. This outlet of Michaels has since moved a few blocks, to more peaceful ground along Airport Way.

13. MARYHILL MUSEUM

"The first thing you need to learn is the difference between Maryhill myths and Maryhill reality," say Lee Musgrave, the media spokesman for Maryhill Museum.

Every year, people come visit this fine arts museum in the desert above the Columbia River, and they insist on the wildest things.

They insist that the builder, railroad magnate Sam Hill, kidnapped Queen Marie of Romania and kept her prisoner in a basement cell. And they insist the museum used to keep the world's largest sturgeon in a basement swimming pool. *And* the queen's gold gown on display in the main hall is covered with real diamonds that the museum staff replace with rhinestones whenever they need money to cover operating expenses. *And* Queen Marie was the lesbian lover of dancer Loie Fuller. *And* the place is haunted. Really haunted. A Druid funeral barge, acquired but never displayed, is still stored in pieces somewhere in the museum. And, and, and . . .

To start with, Lee says, "We don't even *have* a basement."

He explains how the huge Italian villa was built out of poured concrete, with the wooden floors laid over it. As the building heats and cools, it makes a lot of odd noises. He says, "I've been here in this building by myself at night, and I can tell you there are sounds that make you think there's someone in here with you."

Once, a constant knocking from the second floor turned out to be a raven caught between a window and an ornate iron security grille.

About the queen and Loie Fuller, the museum's collections manager, Betty Long, says, "They were very personal. They were very warm. Loie Fuller was gay—that *was* established. She did have a lover. But there was no same-sex relationship between her and Marie."

Ironically, the true stories Betty and Lee offer are better than the rumors. The museum houses royal Romanian court furniture and artifacts, including the pen used to sign the Treaty of Ghent. For years the children and relatives of curators celebrated Christmas in the main hall, using that same priceless throne room furniture, the kids scribbling with the famous pen.

The museum collection includes chunks of the sailing ship *Mayflower*. It has the first Big Bertha shell fired during World War I. And a sizable collection of Rodin sculptures. And Native American artifacts. And Le Theatre de la Mode haute couture mannequins from 1946 Paris. Sure, they've collected a lot of items, but a ghost?

"I'm here at night for hours," Betty says, "and I don't scare easy. But one night I was working late and came downstairs to see Lee. We were alone in the building. I asked him, 'Why were you going up and down in the elevator so much?'"

Sitting here now, Lee laughs and says, "And I told Betty, 'I thought *you* were using the elevator . . .'"

To find Maryhill Museum, take Interstate 84 east for

about two hours to exit 104. Turn left and cross over the Columbia River. Then follow the museum signs. They're open March 15 through November 15, 9:00 to 5:00, seven days a week.

14. SUICIDE BRIDGE

The Vista Avenue Viaduct was built in 1926 to replace the wooden Ford Street Bridge. The arched, reinforced-concrete bridge connects Goose Hollow to Portland Heights and passes over SW Jefferson Street. The bridge's dramatic height—and the five lanes of pavement below it—have made it an inevitable magnet for local jumpers.

15. OSCAR

"At first we weren't allowed to discuss it," says Janet Mahoney, the room division manager for the Columbia Gorge Hotel. "The official policy was: *Oscar does not exist.* Now it's: *Document every occurrence.*"

And document they do, starting from the early 1980s, when the hotel's third floor was renovated and opened to guests for the first time in fifty years.

Built in 1921, the forty-room Columbia Gorge Hotel was an isolated three-hour drive from Portland. That made it a favorite love nest for Hollywood types from noted sex maniacs Clara Bow and Rudolph Valentino to Jane Powell, Myrna Loy, and Shirley Temple. The hotel was dubbed "the Waldorf of the West" but was eventually forgotten and neglected as a retirement home. Restoration started in 1978, and the hotel again became a lovely clifftop retreat for guests including Burt Reynolds, Kevin Costner, Olivia Newton-John, and Terri Garr.

Trouble started a few years after the 1978 restoration, when they reopened the third-floor honeymoon suite. One day, in the few moments the third-floor hallway was empty, something turned every wall sconce upside down. Janet says, "It took the maintenance man half a day to turn them all back."

On another day, she says, "A guest comes in from the parking lot. She slaps her hands down on the counter and demands, 'Is there something I should know about? I just saw a woman with dark hair, in a white gown, throw herself from the tower and disappear.'"

According to Janet, a honeymoon bride in the 1930s killed her husband in the third-floor suite, then jumped from the hotel's tower, landing in the parking lot. Just recently, another honeymoon couple sat in bed and watched a woman in white emerge from their bathroom, stand looking at them for two minutes, and disappear.

All over the third floor, water starts running in the bathrooms while the maids clean. Fires start by themselves in fireplaces. In empty rooms heavy furniture moves up against the door so no one can enter from the hallway.

"Nobody's ever gotten hurt," Janet says. "Nobody's ever had more than the wits scared out of them."

One bartender, Michael, stays over some nights and reports the television turning itself on and off and a phantom hand being placed on her face.

A hotel maid, Millie, nicknamed the spirit or spirits "Oscar" after she started finding flowers left every day in the exact same place on the attic stairs. In the attic, marbles roll out of the shadows. They roll uphill against the slanted floor.

To find the hotel, take Interstate 84 east for about 1.5 hours. Take exit 62 and turn left at the stop sign. Cross back over the freeway, toward the river, and turn left again. The hotel will be between you and the cliffs. It's that yellow building—with the tower.

16. POWELL'S RARE BOOK ROOM

Employees swear that the ghost of Walter Powell, the bookstore's founder, still walks the mezzanine outside the Rose Room. Check for Walter near the drinking fountain. Steve Fidel in publicity says Tuesday nights are the most likely time. Also check out the sculpture of stacked books outside the northwest street door. Inside the carved stone are the ashes of a man who wanted to be buried at Powell's. The canister of his cremains sat on a bookstore shelf for years until it was sealed inside the new sculpture.

(a postcard from 1988)

This year I'm living in a two-story town house at 1623 SW
Montgomery Street—with severed heads and hands hidden in
the back of every kitchen cabinet. Some are male, most are
female.

My roommate, Laurie, works as a window dresser at the
downtown Meier & Frank department store and tells me about
meeting guys and fucking them in the store's big display
windows along SW Fifth Avenue. You have about two feet of
dark, filthy room to maneuver, she says, between the inside wall
and the scenic partition that the mannequins stand in front of.
Beyond the mannequins is nothing but plate glass and a zillion
people walking past. The narrow space limits your sex positions
but it's private. Plus, Laurie says, you get the thrill of rush-hour
crowds waiting for their bus only a couple feet away.

Unless you want to get fired, she says, you can't go too wild
or you'll make the mannequins shake.

When we drink, Laurie tells me about her childhood. How
her mother used to get up every Sunday morning to cook a hot
breakfast. While her mom was busy, Laurie would crawl into bed
with her dozing father and suck his cock. This was every Sunday
morning for years, and after a few gin-and-tonics Laurie can see
how this might color the rest of her life.

At home our severed hands and heads are mannequin
samples, and Laurie shows me how the dummy industry designs
them for each market. Mannequins made for California have
bigger breasts. They're sprayed to look tan. Mannequins made
for Chicago aren't. The creepy clutching hands. Or the bald
heads with high cheekbones and staring glass eyes. We stash
them everywhere. Under the bathroom sink with the extra toilet

paper. In the cabinet with the breakfast cereal. The one time Laurie's dad comes to visit, he goes hunting for coffee filters and almost has a heart attack.

The only mannequin Laurie has all of is a female she calls Constance. Connie's made to sit, with both legs stretched out in front, her knees bent a little. She's made for the Portland demographic: pale and small breasted with a dishwater-brown wig. Laurie dresses her in a pink chiffon gown from the thrift store St. Vincent de Paul on Powell Boulevard. It has yards of flowing pink chiffon that hang down, like angel wings. Up the back of the dress, you can see thick black tire treadmarks that suggest a very ominous end to some prom night.

One Saturday, we're drinking gin-and-tonics before watching the Starlight Parade. The official kickoff event for the annual Rose Festival, the parade features lighted floats and marching bands and starts at dusk, moving through downtown in the dark.

It also features the year's crop of Rose Festival princesses, all of them in pink prom gowns, standing on a float and waving with gloved hands. The more gin-and-tonics we drink, the more important it seems to make a political statement. You know, attack the idea of women as objects on display. We have to put Constance on the boot of Laurie's MG convertible and sneak her into the parade. We have to reveal the Rose Festival for the sexist institution that it is.

Really, we just want our share of the attention.

In the North Park Blocks where the parade assembles, we tell the officials we're part of a local car club but we've missed our entry time because of traffic. Near us, the parade float full of real princesses glares at our dummy with the black tire tracks up her back.

As troublemakers, we cannot be more obvious. But as each official mentions a real car club or a detail like parade entry dues, we latch onto said detail and roll it into our story. Each time we're passed up the ladder to another official, our story has more heft. More validity. Yes, we say, we're with the *Columbia Gorge Car Club*. Yes, we've paid the *$200 entry fee*. As extra proof we show people a map of the parade route that an earlier official has given us.

Our every exhale is a lie.

At the edge of the parade one last official gives us the go-ahead. We're in. We're ready. Heady stuff. Then he warns us, two blocks away is the judges' platform, and if we aren't an official entry, they'll hit us each with a $1,000 fine. And then arrest us for trespassing.

By then, our gin-and-tonic political enthusiasm has worn off. We don't have the spare two grand to risk. But the crowds love Constance and people run out into the street to touch her stiff fiberglass hands. The real princesses glower. Those willing tools of sexism. A block away the police are waiting to catch us, Laurie and me, but for just these few minutes, people wave and smile at us. They laugh and applaud. Despite all the terrible shit we've done, these total strangers seem to really want us here.

Souvenirs: Where You Have to Shop

*T*O GET A MANNEQUIN of your own, check out Grand & Benedict's "Used Annex" at 122 SE Morrison Street. They usually have enough naked dummies for a creepy afternoon in the Twilight Zone. For a cheap souvenir or a relic from Portland's history—we all have that magpie urge to acquire stuff—check my favorite places for finding something unique without spending a ton.

THE "AS-IS" BINS

Officially, this is the Goodwill Outlet Store, but locals have called it "the bins" forever. Come pick through the bins of unsorted, unwashed goods at 8300 SE McLoughlin Boulevard and pay for your new wardrobe by the pound. Phone: 503-230-2076.

PERIODICALS & BOOKS PARADISE

The world's largest store for used magazines is right here at 3315 SE Hawthorne Boulevard. From nudie mags to Sears catalogs, it's waiting for you to spend a rainy day here. Phone: 503-234-6003.

THE REBUILDING CENTER

Here are salvaged chunks of Portland's best buildings, selling for cheap. For doors, lights, masonry ornaments, ironwork, lumber, and plumbing fixtures, go to 3625 N Mississippi Avenue and drool. Phone: 503-331-1877.

RED, WHITE, AND BLUE THRIFT STORE

It's courting death to tell you about every local's favorite used-clothing and junk store. But it's at 19239 SE McLoughlin Boulevard. Phone: 503-655-3444. Good luck with parking.

WACKY WILLY'S SURPLUS

An always changing mix of craft and medical supplies, electronics, toys, sporting goods, and more. Here is your next big art project waiting to happen. One store at 2374 NW Vaughn Street. Another store at 2900 SW Cornelius Pass Road. Phone: 503-525-9211.

(**a postcard** from 1989)

It's August in the Swan Island shipyards, and I'm exploring the inside of an old cruise ship while it sits in dry dock.

The ship is the S.S. *Monterey,* a forgotten passenger liner. She's been mothballed in the Alameda section of San Francisco Bay since the 1960s, until the Matson Lines towed her to Portland for hull work. They'll do just enough work in the United States to allow her to be registered here, then tow her around the world to Finland, where she'll be gutted and refitted for luxury cruises to Hawaii.

The man showing me around is a marine architect named Mark. I met him at a potluck, and Mark told me about living aboard the ship while it was moored at the seawall along NW Front Avenue, waiting for its turn in dry dock. Without fuel or passengers, he says, the ship rides high in the water—so high that when anything from a barge to a canoe goes past, the towering ship will rock from side to side. The white hull is streaked with rust and bird shit, and the staterooms inside are hot and dusty.

As the ship rocks, Mark says, doors swing open and shut. When she was mothballed, china was left on tables in the dining room. Pots and pans were left on the stoves. Now, these things slip and fall to the floor in the middle of the night when Mark's the only person aboard. He sleeps in the ship's old nursery, where murals of Babar the Elephant dance around the walls. He keeps the nursery doors locked. There's no power aboard the ship, so he uses a flashlight to get down the pitch-black passageways to shit outside, in a chemical toilet installed near the faded shuffleboard outlines on deck.

By August this massive hulk of iron and steel has been soaking up heat all summer. She never cools down, and the temperature inside bakes a crust of dried sweat and dust on your skin.

The marine architect, Mark, he thinks I love old ships enough to sleep with him. This is capital-NOT going to happen, but Mark leads me through the security gates and into the huge floating dry dock. He tells me about his viral load, the amount of HIV in his bloodstream, and says how he's nicknamed his last two white blood cells "Huey and Dewey." He's twenty-something. He looks healthy.

We crouch underneath the ship, next to the wooden keel blocks that balance the gigantic baking-hot hull above us. Mark winks and asks if I want to see the "ship's balls."

Instead of an answer, I ask about the huge fans and sheets of plastic that hang inside the ship. Mark says it's asbestos containment and removal. The air is hazy with floating strands. The gray dust coats portholes and stairway railings.

In the ship's ballroom little tables and chairs stand around the edges of a wooden dance floor, warped and buckled into waves from the heat. Planters around the room hold the papery dried stalks and leaves of a tropical jungle, real plants mummified by decades of California summers and rooted dead in potting soil dry as talcum powder. The floor is crunchy with broken china and wine glasses. In the ship's big stainless steel kitchens, the saucepans are streaked with food at least thirty years old. With flashlights we explore the ship's theater and find an upright piano lying on its back.

Up on the bridge Mark shows me the ship's balls. These are two spheres of cast iron that flank the compass. They counteract the magnetic pull of the ship's mass, forward and aft.

In an empty stateroom Mark says that when the ship gets to Finland everything inside will be trashed. The china and furniture and carpet and framed hotelish paintings. The bedspreads and sheets and towels. Mark with his two white blood cells flops down on a dusty bed. The stateroom baking hot, it's the honeymoon suite. The dust is asbestos. In a couple days, Mark will ride his huge dead ship around the world. A rusted hulk getting towed by a tugboat. Without power or fresh water. Alone with just Huey and Dewey.

Flopped there on the honeymoon bed, Mark says if I want anything I should just, you know, take it.

Instead of Mark, I take a shower curtain and a wool blanket, both of them decorated with the *Monterey*'s crest: seven stars circling the letter M.

I slept with that blanket for years.

Unholy Relics:
The Strange Museums Not to Miss

T HE TRUTH IS, I'm a lot more interested in collec-
tors than collections. From Frank Kidd, a man who
had few toys as a kid but now has one of the largest collections in the world, to Stephen Oppenheim, who hung
antique lights as backdrops for 1960s rock concerts and
now sells them, here are nine local museums and a few of
their "curators."

1. THE KIDD TOY MUSEUM

Behind every successful man, you'll find a private obsession. For James DePriest, conductor of the Oregon Symphony, it's LEGO blocks. For former Oregon governor Vic
Atiyeh, it's his souvenirs from the Lewis and Clark Exposition of 1905.

For Frank Kidd—a former Air Force captain, "the
original Captain Kidd," and now the owner of Parts

Distributing, Inc.—it's behind a plain gray door at 1301 SE Grand Avenue.

"I didn't play golf," Frank says. "I didn't drink. And my wife didn't like me chasing women—I had to do *something.*"

In 1965 he bought his first toy, a Richfield oil truck from the 1920s. It's still on display here. Along with it are cast-iron banks, stuffed bears, bicycle emblems, and other souvenirs that now add up to the world's largest private toy collection on public display.

The banks alone are staggering. Cases and cases of them, thousands, including two thousand bought from the famous Mosler Lock collection when it was auctioned in 1982. Plus pieces from the Walter Chrysler collection. The banks are each relics from a specific moment in history. It seems every historical trend or entity—battles, coronations, businesses, prejudices—is marked with a cast-iron bank. Some of them weigh up to fifteen pounds.

"I never go out after a specific toy or bank," Frank says. "It all just fatalistically jumps on my back."

The "Paddy and the Pig" banks feature a caricature of an Irishman who holds a pig. When you make a deposit, the pig kicks the coin into the man's mouth. Here are Jolly Nigger banks in their original wooden boxes. A "Freedman" bank made just after the Civil War features a black man who takes your money, shakes his head no, and thumbs his nose at you. These days, he's worth more than $360,000. Here are banks from the 1840s and even more from the post–Civil War years of the 1860s and 1870s. Some with their Christie's and Sotheby's price tags still hanging on them. "As far as mechanical banks, I've got the best collection on public display in the world," Frank says, "according to me."

He started buying in flea markets and garage sales. "Now it's gotten so competitive I don't go to either one anymore," he says. Instead, he spends as many as 137 days out of every year traveling the world to attend shows and conventions.

Looking at the rows of banks that crowd the shelves around him, Frank says, "Some of these are 'one-ofs.' A lot of these banks are worth more than all the gold coins you could cram into them." And don't miss the little German statue of a woman using a bidet. The way it works, using your body heat, is sheer genius.

The best of Frank's collection is displayed in a wood-paneled room above the parts office on the east side of Grand Avenue, at 1300, under the PARTS DISTRIBUTING, INC. sign. Elsewhere, he has pallets of toys stored, with no room to show them—just the opposite of his childhood, when he remembers having very few toys.

It took him years to get the city's permission to build his museum, but it's open Monday through Friday, 8:00 to 5:30.

2. Stark's Vacuum Cleaner Museum

A few blocks north of the Kidd Toy Museum, don't miss the Vacuum Cleaner Museum. Kill a rainy afternoon here at 107 NE Grand Avenue, but don't forget to wipe your damn feet.

3. MOVIE MADNESS

You want to see the knife that stabbed Vera Miles in the mouth in the movie *Psycho*? How about the knife that cut Drew Barrymore's throat in *Scream,* with the special effects "blood bag" still attached? Well, it's all here at Mike Clark's Movie Madness, 4320 SE Belmont Street. Phone: 503-234-4363.

For the more squeamish, here's Julie Andrews's orange-and-avocado dirndl from *The Sound of Music.* Mike Meyers's lime-green suit from *Austin Powers.* Natalie Wood's blue chiffon shorty dress from *West Side Story.* Tony Curtis's lacy ladies' hat from *Some Like It Hot.* Plus a rubbery "Mugwamp" from 1992's *Naked Lunch.* And tons more, all on display.

4. THE PORTLANDIA EXHIBIT AND PORTLAND VISUAL CHRONICLE

Take the elevator or stairs to the second floor of the Portland Building at SW Fifth Avenue and Main Street. On display you'll find photos of the *Portlandia* statue being delivered on a barge, on October 6, 1985, then being hauled through the streets on a flatbed truck. Also on display is the huge fiberglass mold for the statue's face, modeled after the artist's wife, Sherry Kaskey. A third the size of the Statue of Liberty, the *Portlandia* was created by Raymond Kaskey, using the same hammered copper method.

A favorite local prank is to hang a yo-yo from its huge index finger.

In this same area look for the art collection called the "Portland Visual Chronicle." Since the 1930s, the city's been commissioning artwork that shows urban life. Drawings, photos, paintings, and prints, some of it's on display here in a rotating show that was first created in 1984.

5. THE GALLERIES

To see more of the "Portland Visual Chronicle," PDX gallery owner Jane Beebe says to check out the BICC Gallery at the local medical school, the University of Oregon Health Sciences Center. It hosts a rotating show from the Chronicle.

Jane suggests some other local galleries where you can enjoy art without the crowds. The first Thursday of each month, the downtown galleries stay open late to unveil their new shows. The event is so popular that Jane doesn't open her own gallery because of the crush of people.

For art outside the Pearl District, she says to try the Art Gym at Marylhurst College. The Cooley Gallery at Reed College. Or the Archer Gallery at Clark College across the Columbia River in Vancouver, Washington.

Jane says, "On the national level, there's a 'buzz' about the Portland art scene." She explains that the lower cost of living here has attracted a glut of quality artists from other cities. Unfortunately, the Portland "collecting base" is small, with a big resistance to high prices. This makes for a buyers' market—an overabundance of quality art at low, low prices.

If you're brave enough to gate crash, you might walk into the exclusive "First Wednesday," when Jane says the galleries make their real money. It's the day before each "First Thursday"—usually by invitation only—but few galleries will check you at the door. Really, their biggest concern might be losing their special liquor license if too many of the general public walk in. But, Jane says, "If you come, they probably won't turn you away."

6. Count the Hippos

Hippo Hardware & Trading Company is called the "Holding and Fondling Museum" because of Ralph Jacobson, who ran his Good Used Furniture store for years in the Barber Block on SE Grand Avenue. It was Ralph who taught Hippo partners Stephen Oppenheim and Steve Miller how to fondle something at auction and feel the difference between bronze or brass and worthless pot metal despite layers of paint or rust.

"It really is a handling and fondling business," Oppenheim says.

The store's dancing hippo logo is based on local hairdresser Patty DeAngelo, who loves to roller-skate at Oakes Park Roller Rink. The way the hippo flails with one arm and one leg in the air is how Patty looks as she's thrown free during crack-the-whip. The hippos painted on the columns that line the store along E Burnside Street were done by street artist Andy Olive, who still lives under the freeway on-ramp to Interstate 84 off NE Sixteenth Avenue. They're the only part of the building not marked by graffiti taggers.

"We're protected by the Curse of the Hippo," Oppenheim says. "Since we had them done by a street artist, anyone who ruined them would be known on the street."

Since opening in 1977, Hippo Hardware has been a clearinghouse for chunks of Portland history. Look for light fixtures and architectural details from the Portland Hotel (1890–1951), the Benson Hotel, the Central Library, and City Hall. A gingerbread arch from the Hoyt Hotel hangs in one room. In the past Hippo's also outfitted local movie sets. "The first time we saw Madonna naked, it was under our lights," Oppenheim says, referring to the acupuncture scene from *Body of Evidence.* In *The War of the Roses,* after Kathleen Turner bites Michael Douglas's testicles, he sits on a black bidet that Hippo bought and resold. "If anyone in Portland has a black bidet," he says, "that's the one. There's not a lot of black bidets floating around *this* town."

Kids have counted more than three hundred hippos hiding in the store. Toys, dolls, and statues, Oppenheim says the best is a huge stuffed pink hippo that a well-dressed woman threw at the store one day, shouting, "I've been at yard sales all day, and this is the best thing I could find. Here, it's yours!" before she roared away in her Cadillac.

Oppenheim tells the story of his store's last location, prior to 1991, on SE Twelfth Avenue, the site of three murders and years of poltergeist hijinks. There one day,

Oppenheim saw an old man stumbling down the stairs from the apartments on the second floor. The man was flushed and sweating, trembling as he talked about his first day as a rookie cop in Portland in the 1940s. A couple in the apartment in the south end of the second floor had fought and the wife had dismembered her husband with an ax. In the claw-foot tub she'd stripped the meat from his bones. She'd called her sister, a stripper who danced with a boa constrictor, and said there was enough meat to feed the snake for a year. The stripper sister explained that boas only eat live food and then called the police. The old man, now in his seventies, told Oppenheim how he'd arrived at the murder scene to find blood on the stairs. The second-floor landing was a pool of blood, and the messy skeleton in the claw-foot bathtub was something he'd never forget.

When Oppenheim found the old cop sweating and shaking on the stairs, the man had come back for his first look in forty years. "The bathtub," Oppenheim says, "is still there."

Another night, an employee was alone in the store when a single hanging light on display started to swing. Then another and another, until all the hanging lamps and chandeliers were swinging without a draft to explain it. At that point the employee panicked and left.

In 1991 the store used shopping carts and "the philosophy of leaf-cutter ants" to haul the inventory to the current building at 1040 E Burnside. Still, despite the "Curse of the Hippo," watch your step. Customers tell Oppenheim that his new store is just as haunted.

7. The World's Largest Hair Ball

The Lord does work in very mysterious ways. To see the hair ball—a 2.5-pound wad of calcium and hair, cut from the gut of a three-hundred-pound pig in the 1950s—and the whole collection of deformed and stuffed animals, take an hour and drive south on Interstate 5. Take the Woodburn exit and follow the signs for Highway 99E to Mount Angel. The exhibit is in a self-guided museum at the Benedictine Mount Angel Abbey and Seminary. Not for the queasy.

8. Bob's Red Mill Flour

In 1977, Bob and Charlee Moore were walking near Dufur, Oregon. "Down in this little draw," Bob says, "was a little old building, and I told my wife, 'That's an old flour mill.'"

It was the Dufur White Flour Mill, which operated from 1872 through the 1930s, using millstones that had come around the Cape of Good Hope in 1870. Today, those stones are grinding again, twenty-four hours a day. Turning at 125 rotations per minute, they chew up six hundred pounds of wheat per hour at Bob's Red Mill Flour, 5209 SE International Way. Phone: 503-654-3215.

The Moores started grinding flour on a five-acre farm outside of Redding, California, in the mid-1950s. In 1972 they started commercial milling after Bob read the book *John Goffe's Mill,* by George Woodbury. "I was at the library," Bob says, "and the book was just lying there on the table. It was like some angel pointed it out to me. It really became practical after I read this. I thought, 'I can *do this.*'"

With his square gray beard and eyeglasses, Bob looks like a transplant from the 1800s. With the sense of wonder still in his voice, he says, "We were just enthralled with the fact we could put grain in *here* and get flour out *here.*"

The Moores opened their Portland mill in 1978, but in 1988 a fire destroyed it. Most of his milling equipment was lost, but several tons of grain poured down and buried the century-old millstones from Dufur, saving them. The millstones are four feet in diameter, with the top stone weighing two thousand pounds. They're quartz, quarried forty miles east of Paris in a quarry used since the 1300s for millstones. Only these surviving stones made the trip to the mill's new 50,000-square-foot factory and adjacent distribution center.

Moore's partner, Dennis Gilliam, calls Bob the "foremost authority on stone-grinding in the entire world." Dennis says, "Some people know the history of milling. Some collect the stones. Some run the old mills. But Bob Moore combines all those people." Bob travels to Scotland to study the grind for Scottish oatmeal. He and Dennis meet with home-baking giants like Betty Crocker. "They envy us," Dennis says. "All they do all day is sell white flour, while we might be milling amaranth and millet and flax seeds."

Watch for Bob and Dennis to open a new mill and museum next to their current one. With a waterwheel and historic mills and stones, the museum will make anyone an expert on milling. Not that Bob ever wanted to be an expert . . . "I just wanted to run a little mill where I could retire and drink coffee and talk to customers," he says. "It's like you're in a fog, and you can't see ahead, but you keep walking because you're so curious. You just keep taking step after step after step."

9. THE AMERICAN ADVERTISING MUSEUM

Open Wednesday through Saturday, noon to 4:00, at 211 NW Fifth Avenue. One room features nothing but continuous commercials from the first twenty years of television. It also features the best of the print and TV ads from each year's Cannes International Ad Festival. Phone: 503-226-0000. Or check out www.admuseum.org.

(a postcard from 1991)

When I first got beat up, Gina asked if any of the attackers was named David. She was blaming everything on what she called "the Curse of the Davids."

Gina had met her latest in a long series of men named David through a personals ad. They'd met for coffee, and he seemed sweet, sweet enough that she invited him to her apartment for dinner a few days later. Gina lived on the top floor of the Hadley House Apartments at SW Salmon Street and Twentieth Avenue, and I lived on the second floor. The walls were so thin that on any night I could hear at least three different television shows in the apartments around mine.

The writer Katherine Dunn is right about every corner having a story. I was attacked at the corner of SW Alder Street and Fifth Avenue—it's the Red Star Grill now. I was leaving a gym on a Friday night, just at dusk, and coming around that corner I was jumped by a group of young men. They were black and wore black-hooded sweatshirts, and the first one slammed a fist into the side of my jaw so hard I fell sideways and bounced my head off the sidewalk.

Someone shouted, "Twenty-five points."

After that, every time anyone kicked me in the head or the back, someone shouted, "Ten points." Or they shouted, "Twenty points," if they kicked extra hard or their shoe landed in my face. This all lasted about the length of a traffic light. Then they were running away, and I got up and shouted after them. Then they were chasing me, and I ran for the lights and traffic of W Burnside Street.

That same night Gina's plan was to cook dinner for her latest David. He came over and sat on her sofa, and she gave him a glass of wine to drink while she finished in the kitchen. Her apartment had a kitchen–living room layout where you could still talk to each other but not see from room to room.

When I called the police after my attack, the officer on the phone said I'd screwed up by not going to a hospital for treatment. Something to always keep in mind, walking in downtown Portland. He called it a "wilding incident" and offered to send me a form I could fill out and mail back.

Instead of going to a hospital, I'd called Gina from the telephone booth at NW Fourth Avenue and Davis Street, the little one shaped like a Chinese pagoda.

That same night, it wasn't more than a glass of wine later when Gina had come out of her kitchen. She wore a frilly apron and quilted oven mitts and carried a steaming glass dish of lasagna. Her hair all sprayed in place, her lipstick perfect, she said, "Dinner's ready."

The door from her apartment to the hallway was standing open. It was open, and her latest David was gone. The glass of wine was empty, sitting on the glass coffee table. On the sofa was a copy of *Cosmopolitan* magazine, open to an illustrated article about vaginas. Outside in the hallway stood some old-lady neighbor still holding a sack of garbage and peering in at Gina.

Sprayed across Gina's new sofa were big gobs of fresh sperm.

Gina stood there, smelling her own hairspray and steaming homemade lasagna.

And the old-lady neighbor in the hallway said, "Gina, honey, are you all right?"

It was right then her telephone rang.

That's why I never made it to the hospital. For the next few weeks I couldn't chew with my back teeth. The inside of my cheeks were so bruised and split that I ate everything in nibbles with just my incisors. But that night in the fake pagoda phone booth, when Gina told me her story, her theory about "the Curse of the Davids," the cum still soaking into the sofa beside her, no matter how much it would hurt later, I had to laugh.

Getting Off:
How to Knock Off a Piece in Portland

"THE JIG'S UP—people are having sex in Portland," says Teresa Dulce. An advocate for Portland's sex workers and the publisher of the internationally famous magazine *Danzine,* Teresa says, "Instead of fighting the inevitable, let's try to prevent unwanted pregnancy and disease."

Teresa sits in the Bread and Ink Café on SE Hawthorne Boulevard, eating a salad of asparagus. Her eyes are either brown or green, depending on her mood. Since her car broke down outside of town in 1994, she's been here, writing, editing, and performing as a way to improve working conditions in the sex industry.

With her pale, heart-shaped face, her thick, dark hair tied back, she could be a ballet dancer wearing a long-sleeved, tight black top. With her full Italian lips, Teresa says, "The sky has not fallen when there's been trade before. There are plenty of guys who just want to knock off a piece and are grateful for sex. If there were as many of us getting raped and killed as people say, there wouldn't be a woman left standing on the street."

Ordering a glass of white wine, she adds, "Sex work *does* exist. It's going to exist with or *without* our permission. I'd just like to make it as safe and informed as possible."

According to history, Teresa's right. Sex work has always existed here in Stumptown. In 1912, Portland's Vice Commission investigated the city's 547 hotels, apartment buildings, and rooming houses and found 431 of them to be "Wholly Immoral." Another eighteen of them were iffy. The investigation consisted of sending undercover female agents to each business to look around and interview the managers. The resulting vice report reads like a soft-porn romance novel: scenes of naked young women wandering the halls in fluttering silk kimonos. Described as "voluptuous blondes," they strut around in "lace nightgowns, embroidered Japanese slippers and diamonds." Their workplace—called a bawdy house or parlor house— always seems to be paneled in "Circassian walnut and mirrors" and crammed with Battenberg lace, Victrolas, and cut-glass vases and chandeliers. The famous 1912 report refers to these women by their first names: Mazie, Katherine, Ethel, Edith . . . and says they each served twenty-five to thirty different men every night.

These were famous houses like the Louvre at SW Fifth Avenue and Stark Street. Or the Paris House on the south side of NW Davis Street, between Third and Fourth Avenues, a brothel that boasted "a girl from every nation on Earth." Or the Mansion of Sin run by Madam Lida Fanshaw at SW Broadway and Morrison Street, now the site of the Abercrombie & Fitch clothing store.

Richard Engeman, Public Historian for the Oregon Historical Society, says few of those brothels were documented, but the proof is hidden in official records like the census. "When you find forty women living at the same address, and they're all seamstresses, it's a brothel." He adds, "Sure, they're popping off a lot of buttons, but that doesn't make them seamstresses."

In hot weather street bands used to march through the city, leading men back to the bars near the river, thus "drumming up business." Along their routes working women would lean from windows, advertising what was available.

In the vaudeville theaters the actresses and singers would roam the curtained boxes between their acts on-stage. Called "box rustlers," they sold beer and sex.

Portland police officer Lola Greene Baldwin, the first policewoman in the nation, attacked Portland's venerable department stores, including Meier & Frank, Lippman-Wolfe's, and Olds & King's, on the accusation that easy credit forced many young girls into debt and trading sex for money. She fought to keep young women from being displayed in parades during the Rose Festival and had the touring comedienne Sophie Tucker arrested for public indecency.

In 1912 an estimated three thousand local women worked as prostitutes, so many that Portland mayor Allan

Rushlight campaigned to turn all of Ross Island into a penal colony solely for sex workers.

The moral crusade of 1912 was the city's biggest until the crusade of 1948, and the crusade of 1999, and the crusade of . . . well, you get the point.

It's a business cycle Teresa Dulce's seen since she started dancing at age twenty-three. Pragmatic, frank, and funny, she describes the Portland sex industry in slightly more realistic terms than the vice report.

Free speech is so protected under the Oregon State Constitution that we have the largest number of adult businesses in the nation. And, thanks to our free-speech rights, pretty much any type of no-contact nude performance is legal. According to Teresa, Portland (aka "Pornland") has at least fifty nude dance clubs and twenty lingerie studios and shops with fantasy booths. This means a workforce of as many as fifteen hundred women and men make money performing naked. This means you'll see a much wider range of body types, ages, and races than in any other city.

Nudity and alcohol don't go together in any other state, she says. In most states full nudity is limited to juice bars. But because we mix alcohol and nudity, we can't have legal lap dancing. In Oregon it's table dancing, where the performer can be naked and close up in your face, on a table or stage, but not touching you—and you not touching him or her.

In a local lingerie studio you pay to sit on a couch in a room while a performer models. The performer and you may talk out a fantasy during the session. And you may exercise the option of masturbating. You're paying for time, plus extra for anything above and beyond the performer's normal show. In a "fantasy booth" you pay to watch the performer through a window. You pay by the minute, extra for specific services you want to watch. Teresa's example, a double-anal penetration with dildos, would cost you extra.

According to Teresa, adult films are shot every day in Portland. Telephone sex services thrive. Local live webcams transmit on the Internet. The city's fetish specialists run the gamut from the dungeon dominatrix to the Dairy Queens, lactating women who collect and sell their breast milk. Sex workers range from the "career" women, who stay blond and thin in spinning classes and augment their breasts, to the "survival" or "trade" workers, who work a "track" on the street, trading sex for money or shelter or food or drugs.

Teresa says—irony aside—the best place to find street action is in any of the city's "prostitution-free zones." These include Burnside Street, between the McDonald's at the west end of the track, and Sandy Boulevard at the east end. Also check out Killingsworth Street, Interstate Avenue, and Sandy Boulevard—especially through the Hollywood District.

For escort service, she says, check out the free magazines offered in most nude dance bars. The standard tip to a dancer is a dollar bill but don't be afraid to pay more.

In order to dance nude in a bar, the performers must pay the bar a "stage fee." The dancer also pays an "agency fee" to a booking agency that finds her venues and schedules her appearances. Between the two types of fees, a performer can go home with little or no profit. A situation that Teresa says drives many performers to arrange private dances in hotels or homes after work or between shows.

Started by Teresa in 1995, the magazine *Danzine* collects this professional wisdom that sex workers won't find anywhere else. It teaches workers before they have to learn—and maybe die—from their mistakes. *Danzine* is here to tell you—no, you can't tax deduct your tampons, even if you cut the string and wear them while performing. And yes, always wipe down the brass pole before riding it with your newly shaved coochie. One drop of even dried menstrual blood is enough to transmit hepatitis C or possibly HIV.

Danzine and Teresa also run the "Bad Date Hotline," where sex workers post the details of their shitty "dates" and describe the customers for others to look out for. Bad dates range from the bald driver of the silver Porsche who's HIV positive and demands unprotected vaginal sex to the Honda driver who wears a tie and zaps women with his stun gun.

And the magazine's damn funny. In one feature called "You Know You've Been Stripping Too Long When . . ." Item Number Seven says you're banned from the playground after you teach the local kids how to work the pole. Item Number Ten says you go to the drugstore and automatically pick up your change with your teeth.

Danzine is published twice a year. To buy back issues, write to *Danzine,* P.O. Box 40207, Portland, OR 97240-0207. Or look for it in small-press bookstores and Tower Records and Magazines in the United States, Great Britain, and Canada. Also check out the website, www.danzine.org.

AT 628 E BURNSIDE STREET, Teresa runs Miss Mona's Rack, a store that sells secondhand shoes, clothes, and jewelry, plus razors, condoms, and tampons. It also offers a staggering variety of lubricants, with all profits going to support community job training and risk-reduction programs that teach HIV and other STD prevention.

To date, Teresa says the city continues to increase the size of the prostitution-free zones, in order to arrest more sex workers for trespassing—a worse crime than prostitution. And the city recently tried to impose a raft of licensing regulations on everyone in the sex industry. According to Teresa, the city's effort is first to make money but ultimately to eliminate sex workers. Another irony, since the city also supports growing the local hotel industry and attracting large conventions while denying that conventioneers create and support much of the local sex industry.

It's not realistic to expect every tourist to attend the symphony or the opera at night. Teresa says, "And there are a lot of guys who do go to the symphony, but want a blow job afterward."

In reaction to the new regulations, local sex workers rallied by forming a political action group they called Scarlet Letter. They contacted some seventy escorts through the ads in adult monthly magazines such as *SFX* and lobbied door-to-door in City Hall to convince the government the new law would drive sex workers even further underground, where they'd seek less protection from violence and disease.

On March 8, 2000, after a court battle, Portland's sex workers won an injunction that stops the city from enforcing the law. Now, all the years of organizing fetish parties and magazines have paid off by creating an effective political machine. It's the envy of sex workers nationwide who now want *Danzine*'s help to fight similar laws in their own cities.

With her classic Mona Lisa eyes half hidded, her smoker's deep, sultry voice, Teresa Dulce is another example of writer Katherine Dunn's rule about every Portlander living at least three lives.

"Someday, I want to have a child," Teresa says. "I want to live by my own schedule. And I want to change some laws."

Here's a list of places to get lucky in Portland.

THE ACE OF HEARTS

The ACE of Hearts at 3533 SE Thirty-ninth Avenue is Portland's premier club for swingers. Downstairs, you'll find two dance floors, a fifteen-person hot tub, showers, and a snack bar. Upstairs, you'll have two pool tables, large and small "socializing" rooms, two more hot tubs, and a huge projection TV showing the kind of movies you'd expect. It's open only on Friday and Saturday nights, with single men allowed only on Fridays. Couples and single women are welcome anytime.

Call it an open marriage, a polyamorous lifestyle, or a play party, you'll still need to buy a membership and attend a short orientation meeting before you can fulfill your pool table, multiple-partner, romantic fantasy.

For more information, check out www.aceofhearts.org or call the following numbers: If you're a single male, call 503-321-5027; if you're a single woman or a couple, call 503-727-3580.

BEAR HUNTING

For you fans of big men with hairy backs, aka Bears, the Dirty Duck Pub is the stomping ground for men addicted to hairy men. Hunting season peaks on Saturday nights at 439 NW Third Avenue, at the west end of the Steel Bridge.

CLOSE ENCOUNTERS

Check out Close Encounters, a free social club for "Big Beautiful Women and Big Lovable Teddies"—and the folks who can't help but love them. Talking about weight loss is frowned on here. With about a hundred members in the club, you can expect to meet maybe half of them at the average weekly meeting.

Close Encounters meets every Saturday at 7:00 P.M., at the New Old Lompoc Restaurant and Tavern, 1616 NW Twenty-third Avenue. Phone: 503-225-1855.

CLUB PORTLAND

Portland's last gay bathhouse is the Club Portland, officially called the Continental Hotel Club and Baths, four floors of sticky fun at SW Twelfth Avenue and W Burnside Street. Formerly called the Majestic Hotel, the club features a wide-screen theater for Hollywood feature films on the second floor. The third floor has a murky, dark sex maze full of crotch-high "glory holes." And the fourth floor has a porn theater showing continuous man-on-man smut, plus a stage and sex sling for live performances. Membership is about $20, with lockers and rooms available, starting from $12. Larger hotel-style rooms, with private bathrooms, are also available. So is Internet access and a dry sauna. Hours: always open. Phone: 503-227-9992.

Admission to the Club Portland also gets you into the basement jack-off club, Zippers Down.

COCK ROCK

Local historians say the Lewis and Clark Expedition named this thin towering basalt monolith "Cock Rock" for obvious reasons. Located between Interstate 84 and the Columbia River, a few miles east of Portland, we now discreetly call it "Rooster Rock."

The trails lead out to the clothing-optional beach on Sand Island. Trails through the neighboring woods and secluded clearings in the willow thickets host sex scenes you'll occasionally glimpse—so be warned. Despite park rangers on horseback handing out $300 tickets for lewd behavior, Portlanders still spread their blankets—and so much more—at the base of Cock Rock.

DANCE HALLS

In books from the 1920s like *From the Ballroom and Dance Hall to Hell* and *Tillie from Tillamook,* generations of Portlanders have been warned—so must you be warned.

Too often, the first step to white slavery is the dance step. At dance halls, like the Crystal Ballroom or the Viscount Ballroom, single women are often approached by attractive young men. Called "gray wolves," the only goal of these men is to court and charm you, separate you from your loving family, and take you to Pendelton for a sham marriage. Once back in Portland, you'll find yourself soiled and alone. At this point your charming nonhusband will offer to find you work in one of the local brothels.

Well, you can't say I didn't warn you. Look for some of Portland's best ballroom dancing at "Lindy in the Park," held every Sunday from noon until 2:00 P.M., in good weather. Dancers spread cornmeal on the concrete plaza and practice the lindy hop in the South Park Blocks, behind the Arlene Schnitzer Concert Hall.

The first Sunday of each month, look for Johnny Martin's three-piece swing band and swing dancers at Saturday Market, under the west end of the Burnside Bridge.

For indoor dancing, check out:

The Crystal Ballroom, 1332 W Burnside Street, phone: 503-225-5555, ext. 8810.

The Viscount Ballroom, 724 E Burnside Street, phone: 503-226-3262.

The Melody Ballroom, 615 SE Alder Street, phone: 503-232-2759.

Call each venue for hours and types of music available.

EXOTIC WEDNESDAY

The Jefferson Theater, one of the West Coast's last big-screen porn theaters, offers "Exotic Wednesday" on hump day at 9:00 P.M., admission $8. This isn't so much a movie ticket as it is a one-night, twelve-hour membership in a private club. You're free to cum and go, and come back throughout your twelve hours.

This being a private club, the signs around the lobby warn you that sexual activity may take place. And just in case the wrong Mr. Right wants to get up in your stuff, the signs declare that NO MEANS NO. That, and you must be at least eighteen years old.

Also look for "Video Feed Mondays," when a couple performs for the camera in the upstairs porn-movie studio. A closed-circuit system shows them live on the auditorium's big screen, and the audience gets to direct the cameraman's shots and dictate the sex acts.

On Exotic Wednesday or Nasty Karaoke Night, whatever you call it, at nine o'clock the movie stops and a celebrated local dancer does a set to a half dozen songs on the stage below the screen. Instead of a dancer, sometimes it's a girl-on-girl whipped-cream show or an S & M demonstration. After that, the movie—and so much more—begins.

A crowd of party girls and a drag queen come down the center aisle wearing stretch-velvet dresses. One girl, a big girl with strawberry blond hair piled in a chignon and a fake daisy behind one ear, she jumps up onstage, shouting. Another girl climbs up onstage, and the two make shadows against the huge penis and vagina behind them. They make shadow animals and run a commentary about the gigantic sex action. The blond leans down to an older woman in the front row and says, "Mom? Can you give me the shoes out of my bag?"

To the audience of sixty or seventy people, she says, "Yes, that's my mom, and no, I'm not going to do a sex scene with her. That would be *too Jerry Springer.*"

She puts on the high-heeled platform shoes and says, "Check out these *shoes!*"

The second girl kneels onstage and lifts her black skirt, and the drag queen slaps her exposed ass and labia with a riding crop. The strawberry blond jumps in place, trying to touch the spot where two big-screen erections are sodomizing a woman's stretched asshole. Surrounded by this huge pink genitalia, the blond shouts, "How many of you guys know what 'Russian' is?"

No guys respond.

"You guys don't deal with a lot of escorts, do you?" she says. She shrugs the dress straps off her shoulders, and the tight dress shrinks down to her waist, exposing huge pink breasts that look to be—at least—half covered with nipple.

She squeezes her breasts in both hands, saying how "Russian" means getting off between a woman's breasts. Still squeezing, she says, "I might even let you do it, if you promise not to cum in my eyes."

The drag queen is still spanking the second girl. The movie still towers above them all. Other women in black dresses come and go from the dark auditorium. Men follow them out into the lobby . . . to talk. Couples paw each other in the couples-only section.

The theater owner gives the blond a long chrome flashlight and she works the audience, auctioneer-style, coaxing guy after guy to take the erection out of his pants. "I've got seven boners," she says. "Does anyone want to give me eight?" Like a topless game show host, she says, "You guys want to play a sexual/intellectual game?" Pointing the flashlight at each boner in the audience, she says, "I bet you call your dick something different every day of the week. How about everybody shout out the name you have for your dick?"

In the dark guys shout, "Boner . . . Peter . . . Willy . . ."

By now at least half the theater is openly jerking off. The exception is a group of men sitting together in the back, near the couples-only section. This group of men laugh and talk about their jobs, and the blond comes up the aisle saying, "What? You guys think that just because you're friends sitting together that you can't whip out your dicks and get off?"

More women go onstage, making a shadow play against the big porn. They flicker their shadow tongues against the huge shaved vaginas. They put their shadow arms around the thirty-foot erections. As the movie works toward orgasm—the happy ending of porn—the audience talks to the new women who seem to arrive a few at a time. The strawberry blond kneels on a theater seat and leans over the back toward the man sitting behind her. With one hand she's touching his dick. They talk. It's dark.

A little later, the big blond's in the theater lobby, looking at the covers of porno movies for sale. Other men and women meet, mingle, whatever. Some move on to the couples-only section. The blond adjusts the plastic daisy in her hair as she tells the guy behind the candy counter, "If I can get just thirty hard dicks in there, then I'll be happy."

The Jefferson Theater is at 1232 SW Twelfth Avenue. Phone: 503-223-1846.

The I-Tit-a-Rod Race

Organized by the Portland Cacophony Society, this annual race requires you to visit as many nude dance clubs as possible in a twelve-hour period. You need proof you were there, usually a photo snapped outside near the business sign, and you need to consume one drink in each club. Most players work as teams with a designated driver. With as many as fifty strip clubs to visit, no one's been able to hit more than thirty in a single race.

Kinkfest

This is the annual weekend of workshops and play parties organized by the Portland Leather Alliance (PLA). A recent Kinkfest, hosted at the ACE of Hearts, included seminars such as "Erotic Humiliation and Degradation," "Anal Pleasure for Everyone," and "Saline Inflation." The event is held in the spring, so it won't conflict with the PLA's annual Leather Pride Week in August. For this year's schedule, check out www.pdxleatheralliance.org.

With more than four hundred members, the PLA meets the first Tuesday of each month at 7:00 P.M. at C. C. Slaughter's, 219 NW Davis Street. Many members meet there early, at 6:00 P.M., to have dinner together before the meeting.

LULU'S PERVY PLAYHOUSE

Sorry guys. It's women only for this sexy "play party" held on the second Saturday of each month. For time and location, check out the website www.spirtech.com/ auntie/ lulu.htm.

M & M DANCES

Named for Marv and Marsha, these swingers' dances are held on the fourth Saturday of each month at 8:00 P.M. For details, call 503-285-9523.

STRIPPER BINGO

Also organized on an irregular basis by the Portland Cacophony Society, this game uses bingo cards designed for, well, strip clubs. Instead of numbers and letters, each space is marked with a typical stripper detail. Did she slap her own ass? Did she tweak her nipple? Clean your glasses with her manicured pubic hair? Did he pick up your tip money with his ass? You need to watch for all these little details and mark them off until you can yell "Bingo!" And please, tip the dancers who make all this fun possible.

XES

Located at 415 SW Thirteenth Avenue, XES is a private sex club for men. Inside is a maze of black-painted plywood with nonstop porno playing on monitors mounted overhead. Within the maze you'll find plenty of tiny rooms for privacy, plus a leather sex sling right in the center of things. The only room with a bed is also wired with a video camera so the entire club can watch you in action. The club runs from 7:00 P.M. until 4:00 A.M. and has more than fifteen hundred members who pay about $4.00 for an annual membership, plus $8.00 per visit.

ZIPPERS DOWN

Located in the basement of the Club Portland bathhouse, the "paramilitary" sex club Zippers Down is at 303 SW Twelfth Avenue. Comprising most of the city block, the basement is decorated in army-surplus everything, with barrack bunks and acres of camo netting hung to create the full M.A.S.H. effect. The management has even hauled a real Willies Jeep down here and wired it so the headlights work. Porno plays on monitors overhead, and the fantasy is complete.

A membership fee is required for admission. Hours are noon to 6:00 A.M.

(a postcard from 1992)

Riding my bike, I hear the music and go to look. In the dozen blocks between Lloyd Center and the Steel Bridge, here is the opposite of the Rose Festival Grand Floral Parade.

After the parade on Saturday morning, after the floats are displayed all weekend, this is where they go.

This is a Sunday evening in June, just before dark. And these are the parade floats almost forty-eight hours past their moment of glory. Towed by rusted pickup trucks, towed by flat-bed trucks and tractors, they wind through back streets on their way to a pier in Northwest Portland where they'll be dismantled.

The flowers are wilted and crushed. Tens of thousands of flowers. Roses and carnations, chrysanthemums, zinnias, and daisies. Instead of Rose Festival royalty, beauty queens and civic leaders, now long-haired young guys ride, passing a joint among them. Waving. Middle-aged moms in sweatpants ride, toting babies and surrounded by their toddlers. Waving. The sidewalks are empty. No one's here to wave back. Instead of marching bands, different floats carry suitcase-sized radios blaring head-banger rock music. Gangsta rap music. You can smell the sweet dead flowers and bottles of sweet fortified wine. A fat man and woman sprawl in a red carpet of crushed roses, smoking cigarettes and holding tubs of soda pop so big the woman has to use both hands. You can smell the diapers and marijuana.

The streets around the Oregon Convention Center are empty, and I can ride my bike, weaving around and between the string of doomed parade floats. I don't even have to pedal, from the Lloyd District to the bridge to the piers, it's all downhill. Everyone waves, and I wave back. Their audience of one.

Nature But Better: Gardens Not to Miss

*F*ROM THE ANNUAL ROSE FESTIVAL parade to the International Rose Test Gardens—where Katherine Dunn wandered, inventing the concept for *Geek Love*—Portland is a city of gardens. Some are lumps of nature trapped in town, like Elk Rock Island. Others, like the Maize and the flower-covered parade floats, are very man-made. Most fall somewhere in between.

CITY PARKS, THE LARGEST AND SMALLEST

Portland boasts both the largest and the smallest park in the world. The largest forested municipal park is five-thousand-acre Forest Park. With more than sixty miles of trails, it connects to five other parks and wildlife sanctuaries. Forest Park runs from NW Twenty-ninth Avenue and Upshur Street at the east end to Newberry Road at the west end.

The smallest park is Mill End Park, also called "Leprechaun Park," in the traffic island at SW Front Avenue and

Taylor Street. About the size of a big dinner plate, the park is surrounded by six lanes of heavy traffic.

CLASSICAL CHINESE GARDENS

At NW Third Avenue and Everett Street, enclosing a city block, this is a maze of walled garden rooms, lakes, and pavilions. This Ming Dynasty garden includes more than five hundred tons of rock shipped from China, as well as mature trees donated from throughout the Portland area. Phone: 503-228-8131.

COLUMBIA GORGE GARDENS

The first of these three gardens is an old Italian-style villa and gardens planted deep in the Columbia Gorge. Take Interstate 84 east to exit 28. At the stop sign turn left onto the Old Columbia Gorge Scenic Highway. At 48100 turn right, through the gates of the Sisters of the Eucharist Convent, an order of Franciscan nuns who live in the sprawling estate of an old timber baron. The sisters are friendly, but behave yourself.

Landscaped in the 1920s, the gardens of the Columbia Gorge Hotel include bridges and duck ponds, a 208-foot waterfall, and incredible clifftop views. Take Interstate 84 to exit 62 and turn left at the stop sign. Cross back over the freeway, toward the river, and turn left again.

Be warned: The gardens of Maryhill Museum feature peacocks because those birds kill the rattlesnakes that crawl in from the surrounding desert. Before the museum, the natural spring on this basalt cliff made it a sacred camping spot since prehistoric times. To find Maryhill Museum, take Interstate 84 east to exit 104. Turn left and cross over the Columbia River. Then follow the museum signs.

BERRY BOTANICAL GARDENS

The garden's founder, Rae Selling Berry, traveled the world to gather rare rhododendrons and primroses for her six-acre garden. When she died, developers planned to plow it all under until a group of Rae's friends stepped in to preserve this repository for rare native plants and plant seed at 11505 SW Summerville Road. Phone: 503-636-4114.

BISHOP'S CLOSE AT ELK ROCK

This thirteen-acre estate has been the property of the local Episcopal diocese since 1958. Designed by John Olmsted, the son of Central Park designer Frederick Law Olmsted, it was built to look like a Scottish baronial manor on the cliffs above the Willamette River and was completed in 1914. It's at 11800 SW Military Lane.

ELK ROCK ISLAND

Elk Rock Island is possibly the most beautiful place in Portland—and easily the hardest to find. Take SE McLoughlin Boulevard south from Portland, through Milwaukie. Just past the light at Oregon Street, you'll see signs for River Road. Take the River Road exit and go straight a few blocks until the street (SE Twenty-second Avenue) T's into

Sparrow Street. Turn right on Sparrow Street and park as soon as possible. Parking near the park entrance is almost nonexistent. Walk to the end of Sparrow, crossing under the low railroad trestle. Look for the dirt path near the ELK ROCK ISLAND sign. Take the path through the woods and marsh, and it will lead you out to the island in most weather. During the worst high water, the river cuts around both sides of the island, making it inaccessible to anything but boats.

The island itself is a castle of basalt rising in the Willamette River and topped with an acre of dark, mossy forest. Across the main channel of the Willamette River, you can see the posh homes of Dunthorpe. The faint rush of traffic you might hear is Macadam Avenue on the cliff high over the river.

THE GROTTO

Using dynamite, Servite priests blasted this hole in the basalt side of Rocky Butte, where Mass has been celebrated outdoors since July 16, 1925. At NE Sandy Boulevard and Eighty-fifth Avenue, the sixty acres of gardens and shrines are wrapped in colored lights every December for the Festival of Lights. An outdoor elevator takes you up a cliff to the Priory, where the Servites live.

On the secluded road that connects the Priory to Eighty-second Avenue, look for the small cemetery reserved for grotto priests. Burnt black candles and other grisly leftovers prove this spot is still popular with Satan worshipers.

JAPANESE GARDENS

Designed in 1963, this is one of the oldest Japanese-style gardens in the United States. It includes five traditional themed areas—including a sand garden and water gardens—plus a teahouse and pavilion, and hosts festivals and events almost every month. It's at 611 SW Kingston Avenue. Phone: 503-223-4070. Or check out www.japanesegarden.com.

JOY CREEK GARDENS

A combination nursery, art gallery, and school for landscaping and gardening, Joy Creek also has free homemade chocolate chip cookies—and the area's largest and best privately owned show gardens. They're at 20300 NW Watson Road, in Scappoose. Take Highway 30 west, about 18 miles from downtown Portland. Phone: 503-543-7474. For information about rare plants, free classes, and special events, check out www.joycreek.com.

THE MAIZE

Wait until dark and use flashlights to explore this enormous labyrinth of corn at the Pumpkin Patch, 16511 NW Gillihan Road on Sauvie Island. Take Highway 30 west to the Sauvie Island Bridge.

RECYCLED GARDENS

This is the closest we have to a humane society for plants. Here are shopping bags full of rescued sword ferns. Boxes of salvaged ribbon grass. Pots of iris and miner's lettuce.

Blueberries. Photinia. Honeysuckle. And many plants are huge mature trees or bushes that need a new home.

Here at 6995 NW Cornelius Pass Road, in Hillsboro (phone: 503-757-7502), Recycled Gardens is a fundraising division of Pets Over-Population Prevention Advocates (POPPA). All proceeds go to pay for vouchers people can use to defray the cost of spaying or neutering stray or adopted animals. The director of the gardens, Keni Cyr-Rumble, says about 75 percent of the plants, building materials, and planting products are recycled, reused, or donated. No pesticides are used. Fertilizer comes from the Humane Society's rabbit warren and the barn's resident bats.

Here, every plant has a story behind it. Keni says, "There was a fellow out on Plainview Road who wanted everything out of his yard so he could put in a Japanese-style garden. We took truckload after truckload out of there." Describing how they salvaged trees and plants from an 1860 homestead about to become a strip mall, she says, "We were out there digging while the bulldozers circled us."

Four times each year POPPA opens a gallery in the old barn, offering art, jewelry, and housewares made by local artists who donate 40 percent of sales to the nursery's cause. Twice a year they have a rummage sale. In the fall, after the surrounding filbert orchard is harvested, volunteers glean the remaining nuts and sell them. Volunteers also build the birdhouses and garden furniture. They raise the bonsai trees and teach courses in animal behavior and crafts.

Recycled Gardens is open May through October, Thursday through Sunday. During the off-season they're open Saturdays only. Of course your dogs are welcome, so long as they don't mess with Betsey, the friendly, one-eyed resident dog.

Rooftop Sculpture Garden

At the Mark O. Hatfield Courthouse, SW Third Avenue and Main Street, take the elevators to the ninth floor and walk the length of the floor to the glass alcove on the south end. Outside that door is a garden and gallery of sculpture, called "Law of Nature," by Tom Otterness. The walls are carved with quotes about justice and conscience by writers from Mark Twain to Maya Angelou.

(a postcard from 1995)

"Where you're going, there are huge pits in the floor and broken glass everywhere, so it's important you do what you're told," says Marcie. This is after dark, under the east-side on-ramps for the Morrison Bridge. A block away people are waiting on the sidewalk for tables, for a nice dinner at Montage. Here at SE Belmont Street and Third Avenue, a crowd of men and women wear army-surplus fatigues, disposable Tyvek coveralls, and radiation badges. These people carry military C rations and covered casserole dishes. They cradle warm garlic bread wrapped in tinfoil.

The idea is, we're going to the first potluck after a nuclear holocaust: Portland's semiannual Apocalypse Café.

Marcie says, "I hope nobody has to use the bathroom, because the toilet facilities at the event are a little primitive. They're what you'd expect after the end of civilization."

All we know is to wait here. We each pay Marcie five dollars and get slapped with a biohazard warning sticker. A huge shipping truck pulls up and someone jokes that it's the shuttle to the party.

The big door on the back of the truck rolls up, and Marcie says, "Get in and be quiet." As people climb in, hesitant to go back into the dark depths of the cargo box, Marcie says how illegal this is. At any traffic light, if there are police near enough to hear people talking inside the truck, we'll be busted.

Climbing in, people talk about how illegal aliens suffocate in the back of trucks like this. People sit, crowded together on the metal floor, feeling the truck's diesel engine idle.

Marcie says, "After we park, you need to follow orders." She stands outside the tailgate, ready to pull down the door, saying,

"If you don't stay inside the rows of candles, you could be injured or killed." She says, "I can't stress this too much."

She says, "What we're doing is felony trespassing. If we get caught, and you don't have a photo ID, you'll have to spend a night in jail."

Then she pulls the door shut. Inside the truck's cargo box, it's completely dark. We all jerk and sway together as the truck starts forward in first gear.

A voice says, "Hey, wouldn't it be funny if when they opened the door, we were all dead from carbon monoxide fumes?"

Another voice says, "Oh, yeah, that would be just fucking hilarious."

In the dark everyone sways together, whispering guesses about our route based on right and left turns and the truck's speed as we shift up through the gears. You can smell chili and garlic and fried chicken. When the truck gears down to a stop, we're all quiet, mindful of the police officer who might be just outside.

You can't see your wristwatch. You can't see your hands. The ride seems to go for hours and miles. Then the truck stops again and backs up a little. The door rolls up. Open. To our light-hungry eyes, the candlelight outside is blinding bright, and we follow the trail between candles and deep black concrete holes in the floor. We're in some vast concrete warehouse.

A woman drops her casserole dish, and it breaks on the floor. "Fuck," she says. "It's the end of the world after nuclear annihilation, *and* I broke my hot bean dip."

The rest of us wander back through huge empty rooms where fires burn in rusted trash barrels. The arms and legs of mannequins are wired together and hang overhead, dripping with lighted candles. Gruesome chandeliers. An old eight-millimeter movie projector clatters, showing army training movies and Christian cartoons on one pockmarked wall. There's a buffet of food, and a band is setting up. In the bathrooms every toilet bowl is broken and stuffed with litter and dead rats.

The word is, this is the old Greyhound bus barn under the west end of the Marquam Bridge. Members of the Portland Cacophony Society have cut off the padlocks and connected the power. In another huge concrete room, bowling lanes are outlined with little votive candles. Instead of bowling pins, lovely breakable objets d'art from junk stores— china vases and statues and lamps—are the target at the end of each lane. Nearby are boxes of plates and glasses for you to throw against the concrete walls.

The word is, this whole building is condemned and the bulldozers and wrecking balls will clean up our mess in another week.

The band starts and people are beating on anything metal with scraps of pipe. People run through the maze of concrete rooms, holding flashlights and glowsticks. The deep holes in the floor are the lube pits each bus used to park above for service work. Underground tunnels connect the pits, and it's easy to get lost. Stairs lead up to abandoned offices on the second and third floors, those offices heaped with rotting blankets and human shit. In the spooky dark we discover the dirty needles and dead cigarette lighters of junkies who've given up their turf for the night.

In the main room there's dancing and drinking and plate breaking. There's food and movies. A police helicopter passes over the broken skylights and just keeps going. Right then, somebody rolls a bowling ball, a perfect throw down a candlelit alley, and the ball smashes a lovely hand-painted statue of Miss Piggy.

Getting Around: Planes, Trains, and Automobiles to Meet

*U*NTIL THE NEXT APOCALYPSE CAFÉ—and the next ride in the back of a moving van—here are a few transportation-related people and places. The first, Reverend Charles Linville, is the man who cut the padlocks off the empty Greyhound bus barn and made the party happen. When he's not breaking and entering, he delivers mail out of the University Station Post Office.

JIFFY-MARR—"GET LEGALLY MARRIED IN TEN MINUTES OR LESS OR YOUR MONEY BACK!"

The cool way to get married in Portland used to be the Church of Elvis. Same-sex marriages, group marriages, you could even marry yourself—they were all "legal" at the Church of Elvis, where the minister would charge you five bucks, give you toy rings, and make you swear to her own spooky oath. The fun part you didn't know about.

After the ceremony you were forced to carry a huge sign around the block, dragging tin cans and telling the whole world you were hitched. All of downtown was in on the joke, and people would honk at you, wave and shout. You looked like an idiot, but everyone smiled and waved and loved you.

The Church of Elvis is no more. But no sweat. Enter Reverend Charles Edward Linville and his Our Lady of Eternal Combustion Church, at 1737 SE Miller Street in the Sellwood neighborhood. Phone: 503-232-3504.

There, the Reverend Chuck runs "Jiffy-Marr." With the promise: "Get legally married in ten minutes or less or your money back!"

You can't miss the place. In 1996 several hundred Santa Clauses stood in line, waiting to pass through the metal detector and drink shots of whiskey for breakfast. Above the front door is a painting of Reverend Bill, the resident black Labrador retriever, who's also a registered Universal Life Minister who can perform your marriage.

Parked in the driveway are Reverend Chuck's cars. They include a 1973 Ford Torino, covered in a zillion things that suggest danger and painted with yellow and black warning stripes. There're rifle shells. Busted eyeglasses. A time clock. Broken pieces of mirror. Danger and warning signs. Plus there are dead fish and deer skeletons dug up by Reverend Bill. And there's countless rubber nipples from baby bottles. "People can't resist these," Reverend Chuck says. "You'll see guys in business suits sneak over just to tweak a nipple when nobody's looking." The car's theme is "Things That Can Get You in Trouble." The seats are covered in bobcat fur, with the taxidermied heads still attached.

The Reverend's second car, his "Jesus Chrysler," is a Chrysler Newport Royale, crusted with a bah-zillion rusted doorknobs. Shotgun shells. Clocks. A rusted metal model of the Golden Gate Bridge runs the length of the roof. Next to it is a turbine vent painted and mosaicked with jewels and mirrors until it's a huge crown. The hood's covered with elegant gold-flocked wallpaper. The windshield is topped with a flashing back-lit acrylic sculpture of Christ's face. "People describe it as a nightmare. I wanted to use a lot of sharp pointy things so if people tried to steal parts, they'd bleed for it." Up front, he's hung sleigh bells.

His first art car was a 1967 Chevy Bel Air that he bought for $200 after moving to Portland from Los Angeles in 1983. One of his first jobs here was at the Oregon Humane Society on NE Columbia Boulevard. "I never had to kill anything," he says. But on swing shift he did have to load the incinerator. "At first, you'd handle the animals very reverently, very gently and tenderly, but eventually you end up hard-balling the kittens against the back wall of the incinerator. Summer was the worst. It was cat season, and we'd always have a big stack of more cats than we could burn."

At the same time, Reverend Chuck was sneaking cats and kittens home to his apartment that didn't allow pets. He was running his own ads and finding owners for animals past their sell-by expiration dates. Even the French poodles with bad haircuts. He says, "I brought home a lot of dogs I was too embarrassed to walk in the daylight."

Like everybody, one day he accidentally left a sack lunch on top of his car when he drove to work. That whole commute, people laughed and pointed. After that, he glued a coffee cup to the car roof. And always, people pointed and waved and laughed, trying to get his attention. After that, he glued a coffeemaker, then a waffle iron, then a whole breakfast to his car.

"You've heard of Continental Kits?" he says. "I call this a 'Continental Breakfast Kit.'"

Eventually, the breakfast included real Hostess Twinkies, still wrapped but glued to the car. "I've found a Twinkie will last up to a year if the package isn't breached. And when our neighborhood has an ant problem, they're almost *never* on the Twinkies."

Since then, he says, "Me? I just love to stick crap on cars."

He uses only 100 percent silicone glue. GE and Dap brands are good. Sometimes he drills the car body and bolts things, but in Oregon that means leaks and mildew. "I've caulked the hell out of it, and I still get that delightful basement smell." When it comes to cleaning all those toys and appliances and bones and whatnot, well . . . "If you look close enough, you see—I don't. This is Oregon," he says. "Let the *sky* wash them!" Besides, he loves the different "mutations" each kind of plastic baby head or rubber nipple or crucifix goes through—oozing white crud or cracking—when exposed to years of auto exhaust and weather.

The upside is, "Most people I've talked to with art cars agree: You can get away with more with these cars than you can with a normal car. You can run stoplights. You can park across an intersection. When you reach a four-way stop, hardly anyone ever goes before you."

The downside includes: "Everybody wants to touch and wiggle things." They break off the trophy figures of little gold and silver people bowling, playing baseball, shooting, golfing. "Ninety-nine percent of the reactions are positive, but every once in a while you get a screamer who says, 'I bet that car has AIDS!'" He says, "You can't have a thin skin if you're going to drive these things. You have to expect some vandalism."

Another issue is the bees and hornets attracted to the colors and shiny mirrors so bright they might be a flower garden.

And crows. Chuck has a selection of wild animal lure tapes he got from a hunting store—wild pigs mating, coyotes, crows fighting, bobcats in heat—and he plays them over loudspeakers mounted outside each car. When he plays the crows tape, a flock of crows appears and follows the car like a noisy dark cloud. "I love the speakers," he says, "because you're mutating the environment from two blocks away." If you play the tape called "Red Fox in Distress," every dog in the area barks.

Living in Portland, this sort of acting out just seems natural. The whole city, he says, has a "small man complex."

Adding, "Portland makes up for its small size with its loud and obnoxious behavior."

Instead of animal tapes, he'll play bedwetting hypnosis records from the 1950s: ear-splitting recorded voices that tell every car in the parking lot or freeway, "We love you. We need you. If you wake up and have to go to the bathroom, you'll get up and come back to a nice, clean bed—and then we'll love you even more . . ."

At Christmas he blares mixes of bad Christmas music and calls it "drive-by caroling." Still, all this fucks with Chuck's own sense of reality. "Now when I hear crows, I think: 'Are those *real* crows?' When I hear a siren, I think: 'Is that a *real* cop or just someone like *me?*'"

PETROLIANA

Glenn Zirkle meant well. His idea was to find one old-time gasoline pump and restore it as a gift for his boss, Dick Dyke, at WSCO Petroleum. In 1982 he found his pump. In 1985 he found another. Since then, his collection of "Petroliana" has pretty much taken over the corporate offices at 2929 NW Twenty-ninth Avenue.

Now called the Historical Museum of Early Oil Days, it has at least one of everything you could possibly remember.

Glenn walks you through the earliest pumps, the "blind fuelers" of the 1910s, then the "visibles" of the 1910s through the 1920s. The earliest visible is a Wayne Pump model 492 "Roman or Greek Column pump" built to look like a fluted white column. It's fancy as hell, but any repairs meant rebuilding the whole thing—including the leather gaskets.

"I just started watching for the era of farms with old barns," he says. "They didn't go to town every day, so it was likely they had their own pumps."

"Visibles" provided gas from a ten-gallon, thirty-inch-tall glass tank perched at the top of the pump. First the fuel was pumped, by hand or power, up into the glass tank—like a cylindrical glass fish bowl—which was marked with levels for each gallon. This way the buyer could see the gas. Glenn says, "They'd want to feel like they were getting the amount they were paying for." Then the fuel was gravity-fed down into the car.

Next are the "clock face" pumps from the 1930s. On these, a big hand spins around the face of the pump once for each gallon, and a smaller hand moves slower, keeping track of the total number of gallons. From the 1940s through the 1960s there are the "three-wheel" computer pumps, with three places to record total sale in the days when gas prices ranged from 19 to 30 cents per gallon. After the 1960s higher gas prices led to the "four-wheel" computer pumps.

Besides the pumps, you'll find a hoard of drive-away premiums: toys and dishes, most of them painted with the red Mobil Oil Pegasus. Plus countless antique metal signs and rare items like the porcelain scallop shells that used to sit on each corner of an original Shell gas station roof. A few years ago, Glenn got his best buy when he tracked down a retired worker from the port fuel terminal. This man had taken a load of old service station signs, all of them the baked-porcelain kind that last forever. He'd hauled them up into the mountains around Vernonia to roof a shed with. When Glenn finally found the man, he'd just torn down the old shed and was hauling the antique signs to the dump. "He said, 'You'll *pay* me for those signs?'" Glenn says, "I wound up buying sixty-three assorted signs from him."

When visiting, keep in mind part of the building is still offices. WSCO Petroleum is the fuel distributor that owns the local Astro chain of gas stations, originally called "Tricky Dicky" after president Dick Dyke. Glenn says, "Nixon got in trouble, and away went *that* name." The company's logo, a grinning red-headed kid, is still around town.

THE SPRUCE GOOSE

This airplane, dubbed a "flying lumberyard" by critics, flew just one time: November 2, 1947. Now Howard Hughes's "Spruce Goose" has been reassembled outside of Portland. For more details, check out www.sprucegoose. org, or drive by the Evergreen Aviation Museum at 3850 SE Three Mile Lane in McMinnville, Oregon. Phone: 503-434-4180.

STREET-LEGAL DRAG RACING

If you've got seat belts on your car and a fluid-overflow system for radiator boilovers, you can drag race in Portland. Go to the Portland International Raceway, Wednesday through Friday. For loud cars, up to 103 decibels, races go from 4:00 P.M. to 10:00 P.M. For cars up to 90 decibels, there's late-night racing until 1:00 A.M.

The track is in West Delta Park at 1940 N Victory Boulevard. Phone: 503-823-RACE. Check out the schedule at www.portlandraceway.com.

THE TRAIN YARDS

Portland and railroads, it never stops. For years Portland boasted the world's shortest railroad, running the couple miles from Milwaukie to the east end of the Marquam Bridge. It was called Samtrak because Dick Samuels maintained the rolling stock and his wife, Dawn, was the engineer.

Before that, local kids used to play on an ancient steam locomotive that stood in a flower bed in front of Union Station—until Hollywood property scouts bought the engine and restored it as the "Hooterville Cannonball" for the television series *Petticoat Junction*.

For a look at vintage trains, take SE Seventeenth Avenue, just north of Holgate Boulevard, and turn east on Center Street. Go one block until the street dead-ends at a railroad crossing. Cross the tracks into a large gravel parking lot filled with trucks. Bearing right (southeast), pass through the gravel lot until you come to another railroad crossing. Just beyond that is the partial roundhouse with a small white sign that says BROOKLYN. Park along the one-story building adjacent to the roundhouse. A heavy red door right under the BROOKLYN sign lets you inside.

Inside are steam locomotives as big as houses, being restored by volunteers who love them.

This is the home of the American Freedom Train, engine number SP4449, built in May 1941. It crossed the country as part of the Bicentennial in 1975–76, and it's still red, white, and blue. Come by on a Monday or Wednesday afternoon and look for Harvey Rosener, the man who built the first high-speed graphics card for a network PC and who works on the engine with his fellow "Friends of the 4449." Also, check out the engine's latest trips across the Pacific Northwest on www.4449.com.

The last day I visited, the steam engine for the Spokane, Portland, and Seattle Railroad was also parked in the roundhouse, a double-expansion engine that uses the steam twice. The wheels of these monsters hit most people at chin height. The stock changes but also look for engines from the old Nickel Plate Road, plus European passenger cars and more.

WESTERN ANTIQUE POWERLAND

Larry Leek points out a pile of huge cast-iron columns from the Oregon state capitol building that burned in 1935. Dark and cracked from the heat of the fire, they're here to become part of the Oregon Fire Service Museum. For most of the twentieth century the columns and their fancy cast-iron capitals and bases had been dumped into a local creek as landfill material. "Whatever people don't know what to do with, it comes here. Sometimes it's good. Sometimes it's not so good." The field behind the trolley barn is an organized mix of decaying trolley cars and rail-road parts on pallets. Pointing at a trolley car, all splintered wood and peeling paint, Larry says, "If somebody wants to give you a hundred-year-old car, it's hard to say no."

Take Interstate 5 south from Portland to exit 263, just north of Salem. Turn right at the stop sign and then right again a quarter mile later at the sign for Western Antique Powerland, and you'll be traveling back in time. Here are sixty-two acres of history, a grassroots collection of muse-ums and historical re-creations built and maintained by a half dozen different volunteer groups.

"I started with an old tractor I brought out, and I've been here ever since," Larry says, now the group's presi-dent. "I'm basically what you'd call a scrounger—I like it all."

Here's the Willow Creek Railroad, a miniature railway with over a mile and a half of track. And the original 1870 Southern Pacific depot moved here from Brooks, Oregon.

Here's the Oregon Electric Railway Museum, a band of two hundred members busy restoring trains from around the world. Walk through an open-air car from Aus-tralia. A double-decker car with cramped, five-foot-ten ceilings from Hong Kong. Cars from Los Angeles and San Francisco. They have the two original 1904 trolley cars that ran to the amusement park on top of Council Crest, still with the original hand-painted signs for Jantzen swimwear.

Jack Norton, the superintendent of operations, says how the museum's been around since the 1950s. Their car barn holds nine restored cars, and overhead wires allow them to drive out onto the museum's network of tracks around the grounds. Another barn holds nothing but tractors, including the oldest operating steam tractor in the country, built in 1880. Their newest steam tractor is from 1929, with most built between 1895 and 1915. Ask Larry to show you the creepy 1900 steam engine that a murderer spent his whole life insanely cutting into tiny pieces with a hand hacksaw.

The museum of stationary engines could be a Stephen King nightmare of the Industrial Revolution. Row after row of huge engines loom over you, all of them big thrashing monsters of iron, brass, and steel. Here, Larry can show you a stationary engine that runs on hot air, turning the flywheel to work a Rube Goldberg–looking system of pistons and rods.

Next door is the antique car and truck museum with everything from a very antique hearse to snowplows and the world's biggest monkey wrench collection—more than 1,006 unique monkey wrenches. Be sure to check out the before-and-after photos of the vehicles. They're unbelievable. The first one will be some rusty skeleton in a pile of weeds. The second, showroom quality.

Don't miss the restored 1907 steam-powered sawmill, with the kind of huge spinning blade you'd use to kill a silent movie heroine tied to a log. It's powered by the engine from the abandoned Bumble Bee Tuna Cannery in Astoria. Next to it is the twelve-foot-tall drive wheel of the restored engine from the old B. P. Johns furniture factory that became the John's Landing shopping mall. Next to that is a working blacksmith shop.

And opening soon will be the Oregon Fire Service Museum.

The best time to see everything up and running is the last weekend in July and the first weekend in August, at the annual Great Oregon Steam-Up. For more information, call 503-393-2424.

From trains to tractors to trucks, if you think it's gone—it's here. But keep that under your hat. As Larry says, "OSHA [the Occupational Safety and Health Administration] would have a heart attack if they saw us running all this stuff."

WILLAMETTE SHORE TROLLEY

Ride a century-old, double-decker electric trolley car from downtown Portland, south to Lake Oswego, through some of the area's best scenery. This is the old 1887 line that runs between the RiverPlace development on the Portland waterfront and downtown Lake Oswego, passing through the forested private estates of Dunthorpe, a tunnel, and skirting along the cliffs high above the Willamette River and Elk Rock Island.

Beginning in April, the trolley runs every weekend, adding Thursday and Friday in May. Regular service runs through October. The best runs include the Fourth of July trips that let you watch fireworks launched from Oakes Amusement Park. Also, the December runs follow the fleet of lighted Christmas ships that cruise the river. And the Valentine's Day trips are also very popular. Reservations are very recommended; call 503-697-7436 or 503-222-2226. The southern trolley depot is at 311 N State Street in Lake Oswego; this end of the route has free parking.

U.S.S. *BLUEBACK*

Launched May 16, 1959, the U.S.S. *Blueback* is a diesel-powered, Barbel-class submarine that was home to a crew of eighty-five men for its thirty-one years in service. In Vietnam it dropped Navy SEALs and mined harbors. It arrived in Portland in 1994, decommissioned, after being used in the film *The Hunt for Red October.*

Look for RG Walker, the submarine manager, who says, "The effect we're going for is as if the crew's just left and gone on shore for the day." Food still sits on plates. Dirty dishes are piled in the sink. Razors and personal items lie where they've been dropped on bunks. RG will show you the pull-down screen where they showed movies during each two-month tour at sea. A former submariner, RG says, "On some tour of duty, we went out with just one movie—*West Side Story.* By the time we got back into port, everyone knew every song. They'd all be dancing around, singing, 'I'm a shark! I'm a jet!'"

Really, the best tour is the "Techno Tour," given only on the first Sunday of each month. It's limited to eight people and led by an ex-submariner who has no problems lingering over the most obscure detail. Officially, it's two hours but can last up to four or six if the group is that curious. Buy your $15 tickets early at the front desk. The Techno Tour starts at 10:00 in the morning.

Licensed ham radio operators can broadcast from the on-board radio station.

The *Blueback* resides at the Oregon Museum of Science and Industry (OMSI), at 1945 SE Water Avenue.

(a postcard from 1996)

One side of NE Multnomah Boulevard is lined with Portland police officers in full SWAT gear, Kevlar face shields, and body armor, holding black riot sticks.

The other side of the street is lined with Santa Clauses in red velvet suits and big, white beards. It's the thin blue line versus the fat red line.

This is Portland SantaCon '96. Aka the Red Tide. Aka Santa Rampage. Every year, members of different Cacophony Societies flock to a host city. From Germany, Australia, Ireland, and every state in the U.S., they're here in almost identical Santa suits. All using the name Santa. No one's male or female. No one's young or old. Black or white. This is some 450 Santa Clauses in town for seventy-two hours of special events. From karaoke to roller skating. Political protests to street theater. Strip clubs to Christmas caroling. They jingle sleigh bells and carry spray bottles of Windex, blue window cleaner they use to squirt each other in the mouth.

For window cleaner it tastes just like Bombay Sapphire gin-and-tonic.

This Saturday night the plan is to meet at the Lloyd Center shopping mall and join hands around the huge ice-skating rink. There, the Santas will chant and sing in an effort to manifest the spirit of bad-girl Olympic figure skater Tonya Harding.

It hardly matters that Tonya is still alive.

It *does* matter that the police got here first.

It's a stalemate, the police forming a line along the southern edge of the Lloyd Center—the Santas are facing them across the street, hand-in-hand, in a line along the north edge of Holliday Park. Other Santas have snuck into the mall dressed as shoppers but carrying their red suits and beards in shopping bags. Still, when they duck into fitting rooms and restrooms to change clothes, mall security guards nab and evict them.

Now the line of Santas chant: "Ho, ho, ho! We won't go!"

They do the wave, back and forth from one end of the block to the other, chanting, "Being Santa is not a crime!"

Through a bullhorn, the police say that the Lloyd Center is private property and any Santas who cross the street will go to jail.

And the Santas chant, "One, two, three . . . Merry Christmas!"

Above the police line parents and kids line the railings of the parking garages. It's only six in the evening, but already it's dark and cold enough to see everyone's breath. Cars in the street slow to gridlock, so open-mouthed with surprise that no one honks.

The kids are waiting. The police and Santas are all waiting.

Me, I'm here somewhere, buried inside padding and red velvet. My name is Santa and I've been absorbed. Santa-to-Santa our marching orders come down the line in a gin-scented whisper.

A light-rail train pulls into the station next to the park.

The police lower their Kevlar face shields.

At the signal the herd of Santas breaks rank and starts running. A flood of red headed for the train. To escape for downtown. For drinking and caroling and Chinese food.

And right behind them—behind us—the police give chase.

Animal Acts: When You're Sick of People-Watching

T HE DAY I SPENT with Portland elephant keeper Jeb Barsh, he compared the city to a zoo. Comparing the city government to zookeepers, Jeb said, essentially their job is the same: to keep a population as happy as possible inside a confined area. Portland's size is limited by the Urban Growth Boundary—our cage, so to speak—and somehow we've all got to coexist within this limited space.

Here's a look inside the other zoo, plus a few more animal-related events.

THE ELEPHANT MEN

"Working with elephants is an obsession," says Jeb Barsh. "It sucks you in. Dealing with their psyches is such an honor."

In keeping with Katherine Dunn's theory that every Portlander has three lives, Jeb's an elephant keeper, a writer of songs, fiction, and poetry, and a father to his two-year-old son. He went to Louisiana State University in Baton Rouge, where he wanted to write a children's book about elephants. For research he went to the local zoo to volunteer. That was eleven years ago.

Portland's status as an elephant factory Jeb calls "an accident of nature." In the late 1950s the zoo bought Thonglaw, a highly sexual bull, and four fertile cows, including Belle, who gave birth to Packy in 1962, the first elephant to be born and survive in captivity in forty-three years. Until then, no one knew much about an elephant's pregnancy.

Tom Nelsen, a volunteer in the Elephant House, says, "The veterinarian sat here for three months because we didn't know how long an elephant's gestation period would be."

Thonglaw sired fifteen calves before dying at the age of thirty. The first, Packy, has sired seven, including Rama, the zoo's twenty-year-old bull.

"Elephants are in a crisis on earth," Jeb says. "They're running out of habitat. In the wild an Asian elephant only lives twenty-one years out of a possible seventy." He says, "My job isn't to phantom a perfect world for them. My job is to take where they are and make the best of it. I have to do today what I can do right now."

Jeb has a scar running through his top lip, near the right corner. Movie star handsome, he has longish hair curling over each ear and resting on his collar. He has gray eyes and a rough two-day start to a goatee. Maybe it's his shorts or his muscular legs from hiking and rock climbing, but every couple of seconds a different woman steps up to ask him something.

Between questions, he says, "There's a tendency among those of us who work with animals to disappear into our animals. That's why I like to keep one foot out here among people. To continue to spread the word to people about the mystery and joy of elephants. It's an honor to be here."

He says, "Every day of an elephant's life, it's collecting memories. We just try to keep mixing it up for them so their lives are interesting. They have the largest brains of any mammal on earth. We administer to their heads, not just their bodies. Every day, I know how these seven feel. From those feelings we plan our day."

In the Elephant House, Jeb's staff includes Tom, Bob, and Steve—three very big men. They care for the zoo's seven elephants, three males and four females. The females are social and will hang together, but the males each stay off alone unless it's time to mate. In 2002 the zoo's most famous elephant, Packy, celebrated his fortieth birthday. Krista Swan, the zoo's event coordinator, says, "Picture this fourteen-thousand-pound elephant eating a cake frosted with peanut butter, with raw carrots as candles, while *thousands* of people sing 'Happy Birthday,' all of them wearing huge, floppy elephant ears made of recycled paper." She says, "Elephants communicate by moving their ears. God only knows what Packy thought they were all saying to each other."

Elephants can live for sixty or more years. Keep April 14 free, and you too can wear the big ears and sing to Packy.

The zoo's smallest elephant is Chendra (meaning "Bird of Paradise" in Malay), an Asian elephant who was just a calf when she and her mother raided a Malaysian palm oil plantation. Her mother was shot dead, and Chendra was blinded in one eye and maimed in one leg. She was kept in a children's school until she was too big, then moved to Portland, where the zoo hoped she'd become best friends with Rose-Tu, another female Asian elephant the same age. The problem is, Rose-Tu is the daughter of Me-Tu and Hugo. "Rose-Tu is a brat," Krista says. "And she just harasses Chendra." Rose-Tu's favorite attack is to grab Chendra's tail. She'll hold the tail tight between her rear legs and reach back with her trunk to pluck out the tail's sensitive black hairs.

"At first," Krista says, "people talked about writing a series of children's books about Chendra and her best friend Rose-Tu . . . Then they thought: *maybe not . . .*"

Jeb doesn't worry. "Rose-Tu's a healthy kid," he says. "She's pushing and prodding her environment."

Chendra, he says, is a "pocket elephant," from a land-locked population of genetically unique elephants, and she'll probably be a smaller adult. Her blind eye is filled with pink and white muscle. Her good eye is brown and may turn a bright gold in maturity. She's only one ton, while Rose-Tu at the same age is two tons.

"I don't know why," Jeb says, "but they gave Chendra my birthday, February 20, so she's a Pisces."

About Hugo, Jeb Barsh says, "He's the 'Anti-Packy.' Some people call him 'Hugo the Horrible,' but he's my favorite bull. He's got such an energy field when you're with him. He's like a hot rock!" Jeb says, "He is the truth! He's energy personified! He's a hot daddy! He's a ride in a fast car!"

Hugo was captured in Thailand at about age four, and came to Portland via another zoo and a circus. "Everything I could say about Packy," Jeb says, "you could say the opposite about Hugo."

Hugo has a straight tail. Packy and all his descendants have a genetic trait for crooked tails. As a young elephant the tip of Hugo's trunk—equivalent to a human's thumb—was bitten off, so he's a little clumsy at grabbing items.

Jeb, Tom, Bob, and Steve explain how elephants walk on just the tip of their toes, protecting the sensitive pad in the center of their feet. They can stop a rolling apple without bruising it. Their trunks have forty thousand muscles, and can weigh five hundred pounds and hold five gallons of water. Each elephant has only four teeth, all of them huge. They go through six sets of these teeth and typically die of starvation after wearing out the last set. Up to 80 percent of their communication is via "infrasound," subaudible sounds that for years led people to think elephants had ESP and could read each other's minds.

"An elephant's brain is four and a half times bigger than mine," Jeb says. "It's fifty percent more convoluted, so they're incredible problem solvers." He explains, "The elephant's brain has all these pathways for storing memory. As herbivores they don't need to be 'wily.'" One reason why elephants carry so much memory is because they're so destructive to their environment that they need to constantly know where to find more food.

"They're touchingly similar to human beings," Jeb says. "They show a great deal of affection for each other. They're curious. They stay together as a family unit and won't abandon an elderly member. They even seem to mourn the death of each other."

Asian elephants have been crowded out of their habitat for centuries, and now only forty thousand are left in the world. As a pragmatist, Jeb Barsh talks about Charles Darwin's idea that extinction is a natural, acceptable event. And maybe there is no more place for these huge, charismatic animals that require so many resources to live.

About the Portland zoo, Jeb says, "This isn't utopia, but for them there is *no* utopia left."

AT THE ZOO

If you want to see animals and not people, go to the zoo early and come in the cool spring or fall. According to Krista Swan, event coordinator for the Oregon Zoo, most of the animals are "corpuscular," meaning they're most active at dawn or dusk. Before the zoo opens at nine, the keepers hold the animals backstage while they clean each exhibit. At nine the animals are released into their fresh habitats and are most likely to be active and awake.

Knights Boulevard, in front of the Oregon Zoo, is named for Dr. Richard Knight, a former sailor who ran a drugstore on SW Morrison Street near Third Avenue. For sailing ships a pet was an important mascot, usually a monkey or a parrot. Sailors would leave their pets with Knight and never return for them. In 1885, Knight fenced the vacant lot next to his store, bought a grizzly bear for $75 and a cinnamon bear for $50, named them Brown and Grace, and started a zoo. In 1887 he donated his menagerie to the city, but he still had to feed and clean the animals, which were kept in the cages of a failed traveling circus, on forty acres the city set aside as City Park. By 1893 the park inventory included "3 wheelbarrows, 1 auger (bad order), 1 pump, 6 deer, 5 axes, 1 grindstone, 2 padlocks, 1 force pump, 1 grizzly bear, 300 flower pots, 1 seal."

Unless you want to see crowds of irritable people, do not come to the zoo in the hot summer months. Do not drive your car. Parking is limited and people will circle forever before they park, then buy a ticket and walk through the gate very cranky. Instead, take the westside MAX train. Park downtown, or park in the western suburb park-and-ride lots (in Beaverton or Hillsboro) along the MAX line. Get off at the zoo stop and ride the elevator up. For another good train ride, park at the Washington Park Rose Garden and walk to the hillside zoo train station. You can avoid the crowd and buy your ticket here, then ride the miniature Wild West steam train or the streamlined retro-aluminum Zoo Liner through the forest and into the center of the zoo.

If you can't handle the morning, bring a picnic lunch and a blanket and come for a concert in the evening. After April 1 check out www.oregonzoo.org for each summer season of twenty-five concerts, including artists like Ray Charles, the Cowboy Junkies, and Los Lobos.

Here are some animals you absolutely must meet.

The Penguins: Look for Mochika, a Humbolt penguin who refuses to mate or build a nest despite the keepers' best efforts. Instead, he hangs out in the keepers' kitchen. The keepers wonder if it's because he has a feminine name, but instead of another penguin—male or female—Mochika loves men's black boots. "I mean he *really* likes boots," Krista says. "In the biblical sense, he *knows* boots. You can feed him a fish, but you always have to watch out for your shoes."

The Sea Otters: Look for Thelma and Eddy. Like all southern sea otters from the Monterey Bay Aquarium in California, they're named for characters in John Steinbeck novels. They live on an annual $25,000 diet of fresh mussels, clams, crab, and other shellfish. When they were placed in the new exhibit, keepers thought they were too young to mate. "Then Thelma turned up pregnant," says Krista. Thelma's pup is the first southern sea otter pup to be born and survive in captivity. Now zoos are hounding Portland. "It's a little embarrassing. They keep asking us what we did differently," Krista says. "The truth is, we don't know. We did it without even trying."

The Black Rhinos: Pete and Miadi have been reintroduced to each other after having a baby several years ago. Since then, Miadi flirts: She bumps and rubs against Pete, trying to make him "flamen" and smell her pheromones. "It's when animals, cats included, kind of lift their upper lip and sniff hard," Krista says. It's not until Miadi urinates in his face that Pete chases her. After that, Miadi plays coy and hard to get until Pete gives up. "It's like Miadi's saying, 'You're not going to pay any attention to me? Well, smell my pee!'" Krista says and laughs. "See," she says, still pretending to be Miadi, "I knew you wanted some."

The Monkeys: In the Amazon Flooded Forest, look for J.P., a female howler monkey that jumps on everyone's head the moment they enter the exhibit. Keepers or volunteers, no one knows why, but J.P. has to sit on everyone's head.

Also look for Sweet Tillie, a baby swamp monkey. "She seems to enjoy causing as much trouble as possible," Krista says. Especially when she swings from the tail of the rival colobus monkeys and expects her father to defend her.

And don't miss Charlie the chimpanzee. "Charlie's kind of famous for playing games with the people he likes," Krista says, "and throwing fecal matter at the people he doesn't." He knows a little sign language, and if he likes you, he'll introduce himself. He points at himself and signs the letter *C* with one hand against his chest. If Charlie points to the door that separates his inside and outside areas, he's challenging you to a race. Go ahead and run, but if you run and beat him to the next area, he screams and thrashes with rage.

The Wolves: Look for Marcus, an almost completely black male wolf. But please, Krista says, don't call him by name and *do not howl*. "People go to the exhibit and howl," she says, "and it's really disruptive. This is how wolves communicate. People have no idea what they're saying."

The Sea Lions: Look for Julius and Stella, both Steller's sea lions. You *can* call Julius. "If you call his name," Krista says, "Julius preens and poses. It's as if he knows you're praising him."

The Peacocks: Due to an exploding population of free-roving pea fowl, plus complaints from the neighbors, all the peacocks got tiny vasectomies in 2001. The birds strut and fly, upstaging the concert artists. Krista says, "It was *really* getting out of control."

The Bears: Every year the zoo hosts a "Bear Fair," where people can bring their stuffed teddy bears. Krista says, "At first I thought, *What a stupid idea!* That's not the mission of a zoo." Since then, she's warmed up to the idea because it does teach people specifically about bears. "Did you know sun bears have sticky tongues?" she says. "It's so they can eat ants." The stuffed bears, she tolerates. "Adults with *no children* show up with their stuffed animals—it's just their excuse to carry around their teddy bears in public."

It used to be tradition for the Rose Festival princesses to enter the bear habitat and, well . . . mingle. "In the archives," Krista says, "we have all these pictures of the princesses in the 1940s in the bear grotto. They're all in their high-heeled shoes and tailored suits, hugging and patting the bears on the head." She says the zoo no longer puts the teenaged beauty queens into the exhibit with live grizzlies. "Well," she says, "not unless we really don't like them."

FERAL CAT RACES

On the opening day of the Portland Beavers baseball season, come check out the Feral Cat Alley at PGE Park, at SW Morrison Street at Eighteenth Avenue.

Cardboard cat-shaped cutouts, each one representing a section of the grandstand, race each other the length of the left field wall. Whatever section cheers loudest, their cat wins and someone in that section gets a prize. It's a regular event at the season opener and occurs more and more frequently during other events. The race course is only about a hundred yards, but that's far enough.

Chris Metz, manager of communications for Portland Family Entertainment, says, "You're talking about four overweight, out-of-shape ticket sellers carrying those big cardboard cats."

Ken Puckett, director of operations for PGE Park— who isn't above stopping the race with a cardboard Doberman—tells the story of the real cats gone wild in the stadium.

The nature of a "seating bowl" always attracts vermin, Chris says. People drop food. The rats come. The cats follow. No doubt they've been in the stadium since the first grandstand was built in 1893, back when Tanner Creek used to flood the playing field. The cats were here in 1909 when President Taft spoke, and in 1923 when

Warren G. Harding spoke. When the current twenty-thousand-seat stadium was built in 1926, they were here. For the years 1933 through 1955, when this was a dog-racing track, the cats were here. The cats watched Jack Dempsey fight here. They heard concerts by Elvis Presley, Bob Dylan, David Bowie, and Van Halen. The weeklong Billy Graham revival—the Bob Hope comedy routines—the cats have seen it all from under the grandstands.

"These aren't cats you'd pet," Ken says. "They're mean. A lot of people think they're cuddly, but these are almost like bobcats."

During renovation in 2000 a construction worker killed a resident feral cat, and word got out about the accident. The neighborhood feral cat coalition protested and worked with the stadium to trap the remaining twenty-two feral cats. Of those, Ken says, two were killed because they were too sick. The others got their shots. They got spayed or neutered and spent the next seven months living on a farm outside the city, at a cost of some $1,700 per pussy.

"This is not part of the *Christian* feral cat coalition," Ken says. "There are two coalitions. This is the other one."

With the renovation complete, the cats were released back into the stadium, now equipped with the "Feral Cat Alley," installed under the Fred Meyer Family Deck. At the rate of a pallet per month, Ken says, an automatic feeding station doles out "senior cat blend" cat food. Because so many of the cats are old, he's built a ramp to ADA standards that leads the cats up to their food.

In return, the cats do what cats have always done.

Since 2000 the stadium's eighty-five traps have caught only two field mice. For the price of cat food, the whole place is rat-free. In comparison, Ken says, places like the Rose Garden coliseum pay up to $100,000 a year to control their rats—and fail. "You wait until everyone's gone. Sit in your car in their parking structure," he says, "and you won't believe what you see crawling out of the ivy over there."

As the cats die off, new cats from the Northwest Portland neighborhood migrate to the stadium. Right now, the population is about fifteen, including "Sylvester."

"He's black and white," Ken says, "like Sylvester in the cartoon." Sylvester is there to meet the first people at every ball game. He follows you around. "He was probably somebody's house cat," Ken says, "and he misses people."

So while the Portland Beavers play baseball April through September, while the Portland Timbers play soccer and the Vikings play football, the cats will still be here.

"The cats were here first," Chris says. "They've always been here. This was just the right thing to do."

Doggy Dancing

Kristine Gunter has blond hair tied back in a ponytail, she has pale blue eyes and freckles, and her voice is slightly garbled because she speaks with one cheek full of wiener chunks. "My joke is," she says, "I could *never* get my husband to dance with me—so I got a dog instead."

Kristine and her five-year-old corgi, Rugby, dance to a rockabilly song called "We Really Shouldn't Be Doing This." Her command "between" sends the dog through her legs in one direction. The command "through" sends him through in the other direction. Commands like "spin" and "go by" make the dog pass or circle the handler. "Dance" brings the dog up on its hind legs. "Jump" makes it jump and slap its front paws against the handler's hands.

After each successful step, Kristine spits out a chunk of hot dog as a reward.

The official name is "Canine Musical Freestyle," and Portland dogs haven't stopped dancing since 2001 when Kristine starting giving lessons.

Unlike regular obedience training—where the dog stays to the handler's left—doggy dancing handlers have to prove they can work the dog from every angle or direction. They dance to everything from Strauss waltzes to disco to country-western music. One handler is training her dog to dance to opera. "Ultimately, the goal in freestyle is you want them to cue off a word or a small body motion," Kristine says. "You don't want someone out there shouting commands or doing really obvious body motions."

She and Leah Atwood demonstrate dancing with their dogs. Leah dances with her two-year-old Australian shepherd, Flare, to the song "I Fought the Law (and the Law Won)." In their show routine Flare wears a black bib and silver sheriff's badge. Leah wears a prisoner's striped uniform. As they dance, each time she shoots Flare with her finger, he falls down dead. At the end of the routine Flare takes Leah away in handcuffs.

To find out about pet activities in the Portland area, Kristine recommends checking the NWDogActivities group within Yahoo!Groups on the Internet. The site lists upcoming pet activities and links to a calendar so you can plan your pet's vacation with yours.

To cut a rug with your dog, call Kristine Gunter at 503-788-3152.

With her cheek still stuffed with wieners, she says, "I'm the *only* dog-dancing teacher in town."

Pug Crawl

Beer and dogs make such a great combination. Now throw in a costume contest for pugs, a pug dog kissing booth, and a mob of pug owners with their dogs, and you have the annual Pug Crawl. Look for it around the third week in May, at the Rogue Ales Public House, 1339 NW Flanders Street. Phone 503 222-5910.

Pug Play Day

The last Sunday of each month, a sea of small dogs takes over Irving Park at NE Fremont Drive and Seventh Avenue. Starting around 2:00 P.M., several hundred pug dogs waddle in with their owners. Also welcome are similar small breeds, including chihuahuas, French bulldogs, and Boston terriers. Among the regulars look for Portland author Jim Goad, who wrote *The White Trash Manifesto* and *Shit Magnet,* there with his pug, Cookie.

(a postcard from 1999)

In July of 1995, I sat down with a group of friends and showed them a type-written manuscript called *Fight Club*. We were drinking beer, and I asked everyone to make a wish on the manuscript. Everyone there had said something, done something that went into the story, and it just seemed right they should get a reward.

Nobody made a wish except my friend Ina. She said, "I want to meet Brad Pitt."

A year later, in 1996, the manuscript was a book. That Saturday night I was with friends at the annual falling-star-watching party thrown by Dennis and Linni Stovall, up on Dixie Mountain Road. Someone brought a copy of the local newspaper with an article about the book. My friends Greg and Sara were reading it in the Stovalls' kitchen and started to laugh.

When I asked, "What was so funny?"

They said, "He's following us."

In the article it said how a *Fight Club* movie might be made, starring Edward Norton and Brad Pitt. It turns out my friend Sara dated Brad in high school and went to the prom with him. Her husband, Greg, had been his college roommate.

Two years later the movie was filming in Los Angeles, and I went to watch with some friends. My friend Ina met Brad. Most mornings, we ate breakfast at a place called Eat Well in Santa Monica. Our last morning in town, our waiter came to the table. He'd shaved his head the night before, he told us, so he could work as an extra in a movie they were shooting in San Pedro. A movie called, well, you guess.

A year later, in 1999, a friend and I were flying down to Los Angeles to see a rough cut of the film. In the gate area, in

Portland, we were waiting to board our flight. Near us was a man wearing a fifties-style brimmed hat, a sort-of fedora with a feather in the hatband. I joked to my friend Mike that he should get a hat just like it. A few minutes later, we end up sitting next to this man in the plane. During the two-hour flight I pull out an emergency pocket card and tell Mike how the director, David Fincher, is having parody pocket cards made for the film. The parody cards would show people fighting for oxygen masks and panicking as their plane crashed.

The man next to us, in the hat, we never talked to him.

Two days later, in Los Angeles, David Fincher is driving me around to the ad agencies that are promoting the film's release. At an agency called Paper, Rock, Scissors, David says I've got to meet the man who designed the movie poster.

They bring him in—and it's the man from the plane, the man in the hat. He and I, we just stand there open-mouthed, staring at each other. Sitting next to me on the flight, he'd overheard me talking about the pocket card but didn't speak up. He thought maybe he'd misunderstood, he didn't think it was possible we'd meet in such a random way.

The Shanghai Tunnels: Go Back in Time by Going Underground

Y OU CAN'T COME to Portland and *not* hear stories about the downtown tunnel system.

Michael Culbertson, the concierge at the Benson Hotel, will tell you how kids used to get into the tunnels through an abandoned building a block off the waterfront in Old Town. Remembering his childhood in the 1940s, he says, "There used to be a whole culture down there. Our favorite place was an old, abandoned Chinese restaurant with beautiful ceramic murals. We fixed it up, and that became our clubhouse."

Adam Knobeloch, an engineer at the Freightliner Corporation on Swan Island, will tell you about a trapdoor in the basement of the old Broadway Theater, and how he'd wander lost underground.

Mark Roe, a local archaeologist, talks about the elaborate ivory opium pipes and tiny carved figures found in the tunnels during downtown urban renewal. The tunnels are littered with single shoes and broken glass, he says. Possibly because the local "crimps" shanghaied sailors and kept them prisoner underground by leaving them with only one shoe so they couldn't escape over the layer of broken bottles.

The term *crimp* was originally British slang for "agent." Men like Joseph "Bunco" Kelly, Billy Smith, and Larry Sullivan ran boardinghouses where sailors could eat and sleep between voyages. In return, the crimp had the right to book the sailor's next job and get a fee from the new ship's captain. When the boardinghouse was empty, these crimps weren't above drugging loggers, cowboys, and miners with knockout drops and selling them as sailors. When no one was around to drug, legend has it, the crimps might sell dead men or even wooden cigar store Indians, wrapped in burlap, to desperate ship captains. To get these "sailors" to the waterfront, crimps dragged them through the tunnels.

Rumored to stretch from the West Hills to the river, the tunnels are also supposed to be the hiding place for hoards of Alaskan gold dust—and the tomb of an occasional treasure hunter who opened the wrong door, looking for that gold, and was instantly buried alive by the loose dirt behind that door.

Local historians even talk about a proposed law from the 1920s that would've required all deformed or sick people to travel about downtown using only the tunnels.

On a recent tunnel tour that started in the basement of the Matador, a bar at 1967 W Burnside Street, several men and women gripped a thick rope after signing a long legal liability waiver. Using the rope, a tour guide wearing a cowboy hat pulled them into the underground dark. Down one tunnel, around a corner, the tour found a nurse in a short-skirted white uniform. Kneeling on the stone floor, she shoved a vacuum cleaner hose between the legs of a mannequin. The vacuum roaring, the nurse screamed, "So, you slut, will you use some birth control the next time? You whore!"

From under the mannequin's skirt, the nurse pulls a mass of pink gelatin smeared with tomato ketchup. She throws it at the tour and the dripping mess hits a screaming girl, sticking to her dress for a moment before it slides to the floor. The lights go out, and the rope pulls the tour group down another tunnel, around another corner.

There, a drunk woman in a housedress holds a glass of whiskey and yells, "But I'm a *good mother!* I love my baby! God, *where is my baby?*" Behind her a baby doll turns slowly inside a microwave oven.

Down tunnel after tunnel the rope pulls you past scenes of incest and torture until the last tunnel. There in the pitch dark, a crowd of strangers rush the tour group, groping their breasts and genitals.

The girl who got hit with the fake abortion, that was Ina from the previous chapter, and she's still bitter because the stain never came out. Me, I'm bitter because I didn't get groped.

Did I mention the big *legal waiver* everybody signed?

⚹ ✳ ✹

MILES MORE HISTORICALLY accurate—and scads less dramatic—the shanghai tunnel tour offered by Michael Jones won't leave you with so many stains and bruises. Currently operating through the basement of Hobo's bar and restaurant, 120 NW Third Avenue, Michael's tour has been more than forty years in the making. When he was seven years old, Michael used to visit a man called Dewey Kirkpatrick, the father of Michael's foster brother. Dewey lived in the Lenox Hotel on SW Third Avenue. There, Michael would hound the old men in the lobby for stories about the history of Portland.

One Sunday morning he was pestering the hotel residents with his relentless questions about Portland history. "I'd driven everyone out of the place with my questions except for one man who never, ever talked to me," Michael says. "I called him Captain Grump."

With his wrinkles and his scowl, Captain Grump looked at the little boy. Michael remembers, "He said, 'If you really want to know about the history of Portland, you have to go underground.'"

The old man led the boy down SW Third Avenue to the South Auditorium Urban Renewal District, where a building was being demolished with no barricades or chain-link fencing around it. Captain Grump led Michael down into the basement, to a trapdoor, then down a ladder to an old door. Michael remembers it as solid steel, heavy as the door to a bank vault. It's only now he realizes it was just an oak door covered in tin.

Behind the door was nothing but cold blackness. Michael says, "He said, 'You go through that door,' and he gave me a box of matches."

Captain Grump said, "You go straight and don't make any turns, and you'll get to the waterfront." Then he closed the door, saying, "See ya later, kid."

These were the first matches Michael had ever handled. One, then two, then three matches failed in the dark before he panicked and ran screaming out the door, crashing into Captain Grump.

Dewey Kirkpatrick was furious Michael had left the hotel with a stranger, and he agreed that if the boy would stay off the dangerous city streets, Dewey would help him explore the tunnel system. The tunnels were no longer contiguous, so to give Michael access to different sections, Dewey would move from hotel to hotel every week. "He'd sneak me past the desk clerk to get me into the underground," Michael says. But Dewey never explored the tunnels. "He had a bad leg and walked with a cane. He didn't go with me." Sometimes the hotel elevator went to the basement, sometimes they took the stairs, but they'd find some way into the tunnels that connected to each hotel. Michael went alone, and Dewey felt safe knowing the kid was off the streets.

According to Michael, the Broadway Theater, the Paramount, and the Orpheum all had connections to the tunnel system. "In the flood of 1996 and '97," he says, "a lot of places that thought they had no connections to the waterfront found out otherwise."

Since he was seven, Michael Jones has been exploring and excavating his five-mile network of shanghai tunnels. Now he leads tours to show them off. On a recent tour the Chinese Americans' Citizens Alliance sent eleven members through the tunnels and they told Jones, "Please don't change what you're doing—this is exactly the way it was."

Michael says other tourists *did* ask for a small modification. He says, "There were several of the old Chinese Americans who took the tour and said, 'I can feel the spirits. This place *must* be cleansed.'"

Michael has heard the voices of phantom men and women. He's seen only two spiders in the forty-plus years he's explored under Portland. And one cockroach, but it was a foot long, and he trapped it under a bucket because he knew no one would believe him. "It had to have come off a ship from overseas," he says. "No way was this thing locally grown."

He talks about shanghai prisoners who were locked in holding cells, left standing in water. The Ku Klux Klan met here. So did the immigrant Chinese they persecuted. Ask Michael about Nina, a prostitute who was killed for talking too much about the underground. Also ask him about cannibalism and the tunnel speakeasies of Prohibition.

During volunteer work parties every Wednesday night, members of Northwest Paranormal Investigations help Michael restore the tunnels, and they say the underground is the most haunted place in Oregon. Under the streets of

Portland they say the spirit of a woman roams, searching for her kidnapped daughter. Other spirits still search for their beloved menfolk who were drugged and shanghaied onto sailing ships, never to be seen again. Still more wandering spirits died in the tunnel system and are still looking for their way out.

To see for yourself, put on some sturdy shoes and get ready to walk through the miles of low ceilings, broken furniture, and orphaned boots. You can contact Michael Jones at 503-622-4798, e-mail shanghaitunnels@onemain. com. Or write to the Cascade Geographic Society, P.O. Box 398, Rhododendron, OR 97049.

(**a postcard** from 2000)

Ten days before the end of the millennium, nobody I know
has plans to celebrate. We've all stockpiled bottled water
and canned tuna. As Y2K and the threat of global chaos
gets closer—all those computers crashing—it seems a shame
that everybody's staying home to guard their Sterno for New
Year's Eve.

That day, an ad in the newspaper says the Bagdad Theater
is still available. The Bagdad is an Arabian-style movie palace
leftover from the 1920s. The theater has a print of the movie
Fight Club. This is too much to resist.

Our idea is to hire a staging company to build a dance
floor below the movie screen. The Bagdad is huge inside, with
balconies and red-velvet seats, spooky alcoves, and fountains in
the lobby. It's been restored and converted into a theater-slash-
restaurant. We can hire a lighting company. Turn the place into
a night club. Make it a costume party with everyone coming as
their favorite person from the past century. Serve dinner to
some five hundred people and have a special showing of the
movie. We'd leave dozens of disposable cameras on every table
so people could document the night. Dinner, dancing, prizes, it
seems perfect.

We buy several thousand glowsticks to hand out, just in
case. We blow up thousands of balloons, including thirty-five
silver monsters, big as small cars. The staging company installs
bubble-blowing machines. Special-effects lighting. The DJ is
booked. The invitations go out, and we're set.

On the last day of the twentieth century, I'm on the
sidewalk with a long pole, changing the marquee to read

"Special Secret Party Here Tonight," and an old woman in a cloth coat asks if *Fight Club* has ended its run.

And I'm thinking, *In your dreams.* I'm thinking, *Not your cup of tea, lady?*

She's tiny in her coat and old-lady low heels, and she says, "I've heard very good things about it. I was really wanting to see it."

This won't be my last surprise of the century.

Some things you can't anticipate. When the huge silver balloons bounce out of the balcony, they land in everyone's dinner. From then on, they're lasagna and salad-covered blimps, bouncing against everyone, picking up and smearing food on everything they touch. Bottles and wineglasses fall and break, and the moment a six-foot silver balloon covered with food lands in the broken glass—*boom*—chicken and tomato sauce fly everywhere.

My relatives leave, quickly and politely, before midnight. This is about the same time a group of airline flight attendants rip off their uniforms on the dance floor and starting licking each other's bare chests.

A few minutes before midnight, our special clock for the occasion, it stops.

All of this I find out secondhand. All evening, I'm in the lobby welcoming people or saying good night. Famous people get drunk and fight. Gandhi is stalking Ava Gardner. Hirohito is French-kissing Chairman Mao. There's a three-way between Hugh Hefner and Judy Garland and Albert Einstein happening somewhere in the balcony. Somewhere else, Emma Goldman is smoking dope. Then Ray Bolger leaves, weeping her eyes out. Rosie the Riveter is dancing on a table. People appear and disappear, spattered with tomato sauce and laughing. Every wineglass the restaurant owns gets broken. Every votive candle in a glass holder gets broken. On top of all this mayhem, the bubble machines just keep blowing down bubbles. People dance. The movie plays.

After midnight, my first task for the new millennium is to apologize to the restaurant staff. But they say, it's not a problem. They say this is the kind of party they've always hoped someone would throw at the Bagdad.

Instead of regrets, we have tons of good stories and canned tuna. But the dozens of disposable cameras, they've all disappeared. We're left with memories and not a single picture.

Photo Ops: Get Your Picture Snapped at These Landmarks

*J*UST SO YOU HAVE PROOF you were in Portland . . . here are some swell local places to use as a backdrop when you say "cheese."

THE BOMBER

Yes, a World War II B-17 bomber. It's Lacey's Bomber at 13515 SE McLoughlin Boulevard.

THE CASTLE

At the corner of Glen Echo Avenue and SE River Road stand the crumbling ruins of a very swank medieval-style nightclub, complete with towers and battlements.

GIANT CANDLE

As if you could miss it . . . the world's largest candle is on the north side of Highway 30, at the east end of Scappoose.

Dedicated in 1971, it was renovated in 1997 and its neon flame "burns" night and day.

HARVEY THE GIANT RABBIT

The towering rabbit at Harvey Marine, at 21250 SW Tualatin Valley Highway, started life as a giant gas jockey standing outside a service station until the Columbus Day storm of 1962 blew him over. An expert at fiberglass boat building, Ed Harvey created the rabbit's new head, and according to Portland superstition, waving at the rabbit will save you from a flat tire.

THE NAKED BIKE RACE

As if those narrow bike seats don't hurt enough . . . At the end of the local bicycle-racing season at the Portland International Raceway, the competitors take a final victory lap—naked. Okay, okay, they do wear shoes and helmets.

PAUL BUNYAN

He's a giant concrete statue at the intersection of NE Interstate Avenue and N Denver Avenue.

STONEHENGE

Built by the railroad tycoon Sam Hill as a memorial to World War I casualties, this is a full-sized concrete replica of the original. Take Interstate 84 east from Portland for about two hours to exit 104. Then turn left, going over the Columbia River to Highway 14. Follow the signs to

Stonehenge, a lively place for local pagans during the solstice or eclipses of any kind.

WINDMILL HOUSE

Screw the planning board, the building codes, zoning, and "design review"—it's good to know somebody got to build this giant windmill on their house at SE Ninety-second Avenue and Mill Street.

WORLD'S LARGEST TEN COMMANDMENTS

It's on SW Dosch Road, just off the Beaverton-Hillsdale Highway.

preserving the fringe
(a postcard from 2002)

The trouble with the fringe is, it does tend to unravel. By the time you read this, small parts of it will already be obsolete. People don't live forever. Even places disappear.

My first week living in Portland, in 1980, I called my grandmother for her birthday. This is from a pay phone at the Fred Meyer supermarket on Barbur Boulevard, just downhill from my two-bedroom apartment and stoner roommates. My grandmother and I talk until I have no quarters left, and the operator cuts the line. This is midsentence, and I have no money to call and tell her what's happened.

Instead, I go home and fire up the bong. The big party bowl smokes like a bonfire of dope, and my roommates are in the kitchen, cutting up a little block of hash.

There's a knock on the door, and it's the police.

My grandmother has panicked. Portland's the Big City, and she thinks I was mugged on the pay phone. She's called the police and begged them to make sure I'm okay.

It's impossible the cops don't smell our dope, but all they do is tell me to call home. After a scare like that, the party's over.

This spring, twenty-two years later, I'm writing a check for my grandmother's tombstone. A few stomach pains and she's gone. Like the Church of Elvis and the Van Calvin Mannequin Museum, eventually all we have left are the stories.

Any book is just a collection of short stories, and writing this book, I listened to so many people as they revealed their three lives. Mail carrier—anarchist—minister. Dancer—writer—political organizer. Writer—father—elephant keeper.

As Katherine Dunn says, every corner *does* have a story.

At the corner of NW Vaughn Street and Twenty-eighth Avenue used to stand the world's largest log cabin, built out of old-growth logs, eight feet in diameter. The size of an airplane hangar, it was built for the Lewis and Clark Exposition in 1905. In 1964 it burned in a mysterious fire. According to Portland architect Bing Sheldon, the 405 freeway was supposed to extend out along the route of Saint Helens Road. The only things stopping it were neighborhood protests and the historic log cabin. "The only reason they didn't move it was that it was so bloody big," Bing says. "The rumor is it was more than likely burned down by the Oregon Department of Transportation."

He says, "That's a bit of urban lore, but there are plenty of people who believe that if ODOT didn't burn it down, then they hired someone to."

At the corner of SW Eighteenth Avenue and Taylor—directly behind the PGE Park scoreboard—video director Gray Mayo says you can kayak through the storm sewers downtown. By lowering your kayak through a manhole at that spot, you can navigate now buried Tanner Creek all the way to the Willamette River. Looking at the manhole covers, he warns, "The S means human waste. The W means storm water. I'm pretty sure . . ."

The most I can ever do is to write things down. To remember them. The details. To honor them in some way. This book is not Portland, Oregon. At best, it's a series of moments with interesting people. This year will take me to England, Scotland, France, Italy, and Spain, plus forty American and Canadian cities, but I always come home to Portland.

If this is love or inertia, I don't know, but my friends are here. All my stuff is here. I moved to Portland in 1980 because it rains a lot. I moved from a desert town called Burbank, Washington, where my grandparents had a small farm. I moved to Portland because it's dark and wet, and all my friends from high school moved to Seattle. Because I wanted to meet new people. To hear new stories. That's my job now, to assemble and reassemble the stories I hear until I can call them mine.

I got my wish. What I traded my tonsils for.

It only seems right to end this book with one of my favorite stories:

Lady Elaine Peacock was elected the twenty-ninth empress of the Imperial Sovereign Rose Court in 1987.

As beautiful as Dionne Warwick in her prime, Lady Elaine (aka Elwood Johnson) founded "Peacock in the Park," an annual drag show in the Washington Park Amphitheater. It's still held the last Sunday in June, supposedly the driest day of the year in Portland, and attracts a sellout crowd of thousands.

In 1988, when Lady Elaine was to relinquish her crown to a new empress, she and her mother, Audria M. Edwards, did a mother-and-son, song-and-dance production number in matching gowns.

According to Walter Cole (aka Darcelle XV), this was onstage in the Egyptian Ballroom of the Masonic Temple, now part of the art museum at 1219 SW Park Avenue. There, Walter says Audria collapsed at the end of the number and was rushed to the hospital. She died of a heart attack, while her son was still performing. "It was overwhelming," Walter says. "The atmosphere was totally heavy. We knew she was dead, but Peacock was determined to go on. She lasted right through to the end."

So much of this book isn't part of Portland's official history, but it should be.

Elwood Johnson died of AIDS in 1993, but the Audria M. Edwards Scholarship Fund that he established is still supported by his other legacy, the annual "Peacock in the Park" show. The last Sunday each June, the show still starts at 3:30 P.M.

About the Author

CHUCK PALAHNIUK is the author of six novels, including the bestsellers *Fight Club, Choke,* and *Lullaby.* His latest novel is *Diary.*

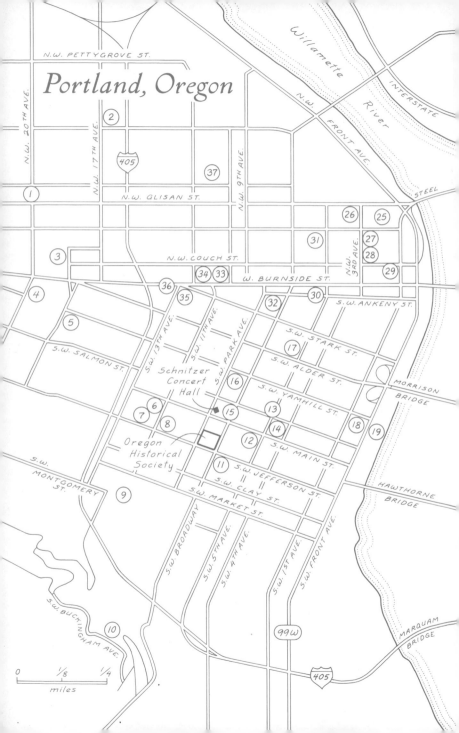